D0380766

SNOW SENSE

A Guide to Evaluating
Snow Avalanche Hazard

by:

Jill A. Fredston and Doug Fesler

Alaska Mountain Safety Center, Inc.
Anchorage, Alaska

Book layout by Ruth Ann Dickie
Earlier edition design and illustrations by Laura Larson

All photographs by Doug Fesler or Jill Fredston unless otherwise
indicated.

Cover photograph by Jo Jo Smith: Slab avalanche in Highland
Bowl, Colorado. Series of avalanche release photographs available for purchase, contact P.O. Box 600, Aspen, CO, 81612.

Back cover photograph: Investigating a fracture line in the Chugach
Mountains, Alaska.

Produced/distributed by:
Alaska Mountain Safety Center, Inc.
9140 Brewsters Drive
Anchorage, Alaska, 99516
(907) 345-3566

Revised and updated, 1994, Fourth edition, ISBN 0-9643994-0-7
(Previously ISBN 0-9616003-0-6, 1984-1988)

NOTE: *All conversions between English and Metric units in this
book are approximations only.*

Printed in Alaska

PRINTED ON
RECYCLED PAPER

TABLE OF CONTENTS

Page

Preface ii

Acknowledgements ii

Introduction 1

Principal Types of Avalanches 3

The Avalanche Hazard Evaluation Process 10

Is the Terrain Capable of Producing an Avalanche? 14

Could the Snow Slide? 26

Is the Weather Contributing to Instability? 68

What are your Alternatives and their Possible Consequences? 79

Decision-making: Using the Avalanche Hazard
Evaluation Checklist 85

Travelling Smart: Route Selection and Safe Travel Principles 91

Putting it all Together: Maximizing Your Safety
in Avalanche Terrain 98

Looking Ahead 101

Additional Information: Avalanche Rescue 102

Resources For Further Learning 114

PREFACE

This book is intended for skiers, mountaineers, snowboarders, snowmobilers, snowshoers, guides, rangers, rescue team members, and others who travel or work in avalanche country. Our goal is to help you as a backcountry traveller learn to recognize, evaluate, and avoid potential snow avalanche hazards.

A snow avalanche is a mass of snow moving downslope which may also contain ice, soil, rocks, or other debris. Because the majority of avalanche accidents result from human-triggered slab releases, the focus of this book is on slab avalanches.

Avalanches do not happen by accident, they occur for particular reasons. We firmly believe that while even the most experienced can make errors in their assessment of snow stability, a large number of avalanche accidents can be avoided by learning to detect clues and integrate key pieces of information. *Snow Sense* provides a framework for evaluating avalanche hazard. It is not a substitute for field experience. If you want to learn about dragons, you need to go to the den of the dragons . . .but sometimes a dragon book helps.

ACKNOWLEDGEMENTS

This book would not have been possible without the influence and support of many people. Very special thanks are gratefully extended to Arthur and Elinor Fredston as well as Raphael and Jane Bernstein. Like a tree that starts from a seed, many of the ideas in *Snow Sense* were planted by others over the years. Foremost among the seed planters were Dave Hendrickson, Ed LaChapelle, Art Mears, Rod Newcomb, Chuck O'Leary, Ron Perla, Kent Saxton, Peter Schaerer, and Norm Wilson. Every orchard needs cultivators to keep the seeds alive. We have had the help of more people than we can mention here, but we would particularly like to thank Betsy Armstrong, Dick Armstrong, Dale Atkins, Don Bachman, Reid Bahnson, Gary Bocarde, Karen Cafmeyer, Nan Elliot, Sue Ferguson, Janis Fleischman, Geoff Freer, the late Dale Gallagher, Bill Glude, Jim Hale, Pam Speers Hayes, David Hickok, Clair Israelson, Art Judson, Pete Martinelli, Rich Marriott, Dave McClung, Brad Meiklejohn, Nick Parker, Chris Stethem, Ellen Toll, Bruce Tremper, and Knox Williams for their encouragement, generosity, ideas, and critical feedback.

INTRODUCTION

In the United States between 1950-51 and 1992-93, 420 people are known to have died in 310 separate snow avalanche incidents. Four out of five, or 80% were recreationists and of these, roughly 75% were travelling in the backcountry. A majority of the victims triggered the avalanches that killed them. In Canada between 1979-80 and 1993-94, 97 avalanche fatalities occurred. All but two of these people died pursuing recreational activities. A greater number of fatalities occurred in Europe, with 728 deaths in 12 countries between 1985-86 and 1990-91, but the types and causes of accidents were often very similar. These numbers represent *just* the fatalities in selected countries. Hundreds more incidents occur worldwide each year in which people trigger, are caught, partly buried, buried, and/or injured in avalanches.

The number of avalanche accidents continues to climb as winter backcountry use and skill levels increase, available equipment improves, and "limits" get pushed. Backcountry skiers and mountaineers lead the list of those getting caught although during the 1993-1994 season, most of the fatalities in North America were snowmachiners. A rise in incidents involving snowboarders is expected as the sport continues to gain in popularity.

These statistics are not meant to intimidate, but to educate. **Most of the avalanches catching people are triggered by people, and the same mistakes are being made repeatedly.** While some accidents are a result of not recognizing potential hazard, most accidents occur because the victims either underestimate the hazard or overestimate their ability to deal with it, often exercising poor route selection or choice of timing. Many of the accidents involve "experienced" skiers or mountain travellers. There is a tendency to assume that these people are also experts at evaluating avalanche hazard but this is often not the case.

Nearly all avalanche accidents can be avoided. The clues are there. The key is to learn to read "nature's billboards." Usually when avalanche accidents are investigated, it is found that not just one or two clues were overlooked or ignored but three, or four, or five clues by the time the group got into trouble. Few people would choose to cross a busy four-lane highway without listening for the traffic or looking both ways. Similarly, travelling on or near steep, snow-covered slopes without gathering and integrating information about the current stability of the snow is like wearing earplugs and blinders.

Steep slopes can be negotiated safely but it is a matter of timing. When the fish are running, some people go fishing. When the avalanches are running, it is more important than ever to carefully evaluate snow stability and choose good routes every step of the way. There will be some days when only lower angle slopes can be travelled safely and slopes with angles steeper than roughly 35° need to be avoided. There will be other days when you can safely travel on everything in sight, no matter what the angle.

The snowpack is stable most of the time and because of this, it is common to travel to a particular spot in avalanche terrain many times without seeing any avalanches. As a result, we get "positive reinforcement," that is, we begin to think of an area as safe. But if we travel to that spot often enough, sooner or later we will be there when the snow is unstable and it may catch us offguard. To travel safely in dragon country, you need to think like a dragon. Learn where they live and feed, when they sleep, and what fires them to life.

PRINCIPAL TYPES OF AVALANCHES

Avalanches come in all shapes and sizes. Even the smallest can result in harm if you happen to be in the wrong place at the wrong time. The four main types of avalanche threats are loose snow slides, slab avalanches, cornice collapses, and ice avalanches. Of these, slab avalanches catch the greatest number of backcountry travellers, in part because they occur on terrain that is frequented by backcountry travellers and involve snow that fails catastrophically across a relatively large area.

LOOSE SNOW SLIDES

Loose snow slides, also called point re- leases, start with a small amount of *cohesionless* snow and typically pick up more snow as they descend. From a distance, they appear to start at a point and fan out into a triangle. They usually are small, involving only upper layers of snow, but they are capable of being quite large and destructive depending upon how much ma-

Loose snow avalanches originating from sun-warmed snow near rocks.

terial they entrain. To ice climbers and other backcountry travellers, they are particularly hazardous when the consequences of being swept off a stance onto rough terrain are serious. The stress of the moving snow in a loose snow slide can also trigger larger and deeper slab releases. Loose snow releases occur most often on steep slopes (generally 35°+) during or shortly after a snowstorm or during warming events caused by rain, rising temperatures, or solar radiation.

SLAB AVALANCHES

Slab avalanches occur when one or more layers of *cohesive* snow break away as a unit. As the slab travels downslope, it splits up into smaller blocks or clods. The upper boundary of the slab is called the *fracture line or crown face*. The area immediately above this is referred to as the *crown*. The sides of the slab are called the *flanks* and the bottom

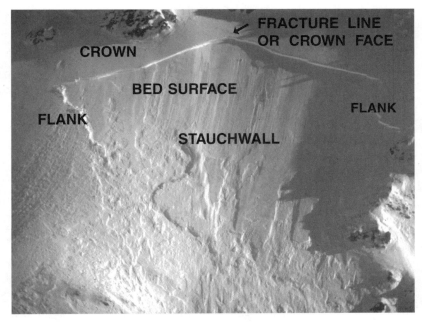

Slab avalanche nomenclature.   *(Photo by Chuck O'Leary)*

boundary, the *stauchwall*. The main sliding surface under the slab is called the *bed surface*. Remembering these terms is much less important than recognizing that the bed surface is a *critical* boundary because it typically has a surface area roughly 100 times greater than the surface area of all of the other boundary regions combined. Slab failure is commonly initiated when the bond between the slab and the bed surface fails, thus placing tremendous stress on the other boundary regions which, in turn, are unable to hold the slab in place.

Slab thickness can range from less than an inch to 35 feet (11 meters) or more. Human-triggered slabs are generally less than 5 feet (1.5 meters) deep, with many less than 2 feet (.6 meters). **How deep a slab has to be to be dangerous depends entirely upon the consequences of getting caught.** Mountaineers in exposed terrain have been killed by slabs only a few inches thick. The depth of any given fracture line will vary tremendously depending upon snow distribution. Slabs can range in width from a few yards to well over a mile.

Slab material is also highly variable. Slabs may be hard or soft, wet or dry. The density of the snow involved as well as the configuration of the avalanche path (e.g., roughness, shape, and total vertical drop) affect the velocity of moving slabs. Wet slabs can move at speeds of roughly <20-65 mph (<10-35 meters/second) while fast-moving dry slides can have speeds ranging from about 45-150 mph (20-70 meters/second).

Several special types of slab avalanches deserve mention. The first are *glide crack failures* which involve release of the entire snowpack on the ground. Glide cracks are tensile cracks that typically open at varying rates of speed (usually days and weeks) in warm, homogenous, deep snowpacks that lack marked discontinuities in layering. They are generally found in areas with smooth ground surfaces such as grass or rock slabs that are well lubricated with free water from snowmelt, rain, or groundwater. Glide cracks are formed as the entire snowpack slips or glides downslope. Glide failure may or may not occur depending on the rate and amount of deformation. Glide cracks look dangerous and certainly, the area around and below these cracks should be avoided as it is difficult to predict if or when the snow will fail. Often, however, the snowpack in the general vicinity is quite strong as in order for the snowpack to flow as a unit it must be well-bonded, with no major weak layers.

Another variety of slab avalanche are *roof avalanches* which have injured, buried, and killed a number of people, crushed vehicles, and caused other damage. These commonly occur on roofs with angles of 20-30 degrees or greater but may occur on roofs of only 10-15 degrees if they have smooth sliding surfaces such as metal or plastic. Slabs usually release full-depth, that is, to the roof surface. Failure is commonly precipitated by loading or warming events.

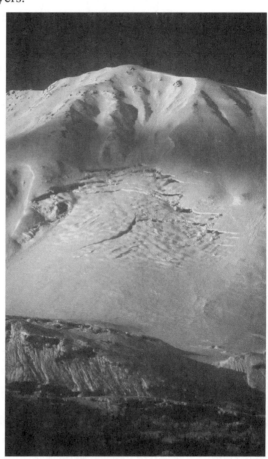

These glide cracks developed on a well-lubricated, grassy slope during several weeks of relatively warm weather.

Slush flows are slab releases of water-saturated snow which occur mostly in high latitude areas such as northern Norway and the Brooks Range in Alaska where the snowpack is subjected to rapid, intense warming in late May/early June. They initiate on low slope angles, often in creek beds with angles of less than 15°. Slush flows are not to be confused with wet snow releases which commonly occur at lower latitudes in response to mid-winter thaws or springtime solar radiation.

This slush flow in Alaska's Brooks Range was triggered in late May by a small loose snow avalanche impacting the water-saturated snow in the creekbed. The slush flow ran approximately 3/4 of a mile (1.2 km), reached speeds of up to 40 mph (18 meters/second), and entrained very large boulders.

CORNICE COLLAPSES

Cornices form when windblown snow builds out horizontally at sharp terrain breaks such as ridgecrests and the sides of gullies. These cornices can break off well back from their edges. They often trigger bigger slides when they hit the wind-loaded, pillowed area on the slope below. In addition, cornice crevasses are often associated with cornices. These are cracks which form between the snow which is well anchored to the ridge and that which is free-hanging and thus more easily deformed. Cornice crevasses may be covered by new or wind-deposited snow and may not be readily visible.

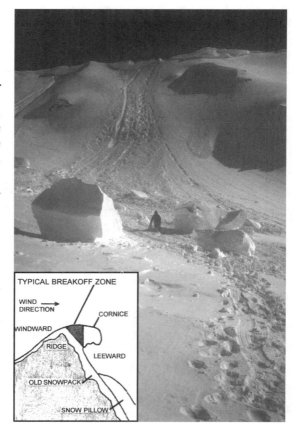

TYPICAL BREAKOFF ZONE

WIND DIRECTION

WINDWARD

RIDGE

CORNICE

LEEWARD

OLD SNOWPACK

SNOW PILLOW

These large cornice blocks bounced, and slid nearly 800 vertical feet (244 m). Acting much like a rockfall, cornice blocks can veer off the fall line by more than 30°. The block on the left alone weighs roughly 64,000 pounds (29,030 kg). The snowpack on the slope below was so stable that even "bombs" this size did not trigger deep slab releases. Inset shows basic nomenclature associated with cornices.

ICE AVALANCHES

Ice avalanches are caused by the collapse of unstable ice blocks (seracs) from a steep or overhanging part of a glacier. Ice avalanches can entrain a considerable amount of rock, ice, and snow and travel long distances. Potential ice avalanche hazard is relatively easy to recognize. However, ice avalanches are generally unpredictable because imminent ice falls cannot readily be detected. Contrary to popular belief, they do not occur at regular intervals which can be timed or during particular periods of the day. In regions of the world where tidewater glaciers exist, there is the additional threat of surge waves caused by ice avalanches (i.e., calving events). If you are travelling in areas with ice avalanche threat, be willing to accept a higher level of risk. Travel as quickly as possible in order to minimize your exposure time.

Initiated by the collapse of a large serac, this high speed ice avalanche off of Mt. Hunter in the Alaska Range generated a powderblast that "dusted" an occupied camp more than a mile and a half (2.4 km) away. (Photo by Gary Bocarde)

THE AVALANCHE HAZARD
EVALUATION PROCESS

SEEKING INFORMATION

Many years ago in India, there were four men who were blind. As they travelled in the forest, they came upon a large elephant. Never having encountered an elephant before, each man set about trying to examine and analyze what nature of beast was before them. One man touched a leg and concluded that an elephant must be very much like a tree trunk. Another man felt the tail and explained that an elephant must be like a rope. The third man stood by the ear as it moved back and forth and concluded that an elephant must be like a fan. The fourth man felt his way around the entire body and decided that an elephant is something enormous, almost without beginning or end.

This fable is not unlike the situation a backcountry traveler is faced with in attempting to evaluate potential avalanche hazard. **An incomplete examination of available data leads to erroneous conclusions concerning the degree of hazard present.** And the data in and of itself is not as important as the *interrelationship* of the data. Generally, no single piece of information will tell the whole story. But what information do we need?

The interaction of three critical variables--the snowpack, weather, and terrain -- determines whether or not an avalanche is possible. However, to determine whether an avalanche *hazard* exists, we must add an important fourth variable, us. Without the presence of people or property, there is no hazard.

All the information needed to evaluate potential avalanche hazard comes from these four variables and is generally available to you through observations and tests. **The bottom line is that your hazard evaluation decisions are only as good as the data you seek, integrate, and act upon.** As you travel through the mountains, choosing routes or campsites, you need to answer the following four critical questions:

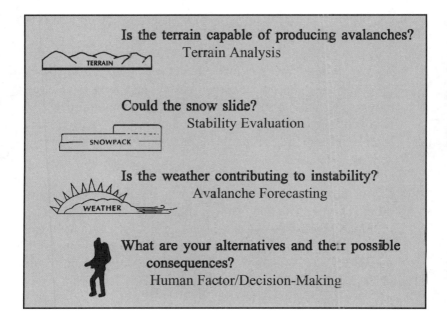

Is the terrain capable of producing avalanches?
Terrain Analysis

TERRAIN

Could the snow slide?
Stability Evaluation

SNOWPACK

Is the weather contributing to instability?
Avalanche Forecasting

WEATHER

What are your alternatives and their possible consequences?
Human Factor/Decision-Making

The first step is to learn to recognize avalanche terrain because then you can make a conscious decision about whether or not you want to expose yourself to possible hazard. If you decide that you do want to travel on or near steep slopes then you must seek the critical information needed to answer these questions. By doing so, you can begin to base your hazard evaluation upon solid facts rather than assumptions, feelings, guesses, or fate.

Is it safe or is it unsafe? The essential problem you are faced with is one of uncertainty. The key to eliminating or reducing this uncertainty lies in gathering meaningful information upon which you can base your evaluation. This process, called the *bull's-eye approach,* means getting to the heart of the problem quickly without getting bogged down by irrelevant information. The avalanche hazard evaluation process should start *before* you leave on your proposed trip:

❋ Begin by formulating an opinion about the potential hazard based upon available data such as local weather and snow advisories, topography, and personal observations. As you approach the area you'll be travelling in, look for clues pointing to important recent events such as strong winds, new snowfall, and avalanche activity.

❋ As you travel, continually fine-tune your opinion by seeking additional key information that will either support or refute it. Key information or bull's-eye data is that which has a high degree of certainty in its message. Some of the most unambiguous information available is in the form of clues provided by nature. These clues reflect ongoing physical processes that affect snow stability. Stay constantly alert for clues.

❋ Be objective. Don't let your desire to reach a goal interfere with your evaluation. Remember, that hazard evaluation is not an event, it is a continuous process.

THE BULL'S-EYE APPROACH

Within this circle exists *all* of the information available to you whether useful or meaningless. The marginal information does little or nothing to reduce your uncertainty about the stability of a given slope. Examples: a) the air temperature is 32°F (0°C), b) the snow depth is 3.5 feet (1.1 meters), c) the slope is 800 feet high (244 meters), and d) the snow is white.

Within the smaller circle exists more *relevant* data which provides you with meaningful information but still leaves you with some uncertainty about the actual level of hazard. Examples: a) the air temperature was -4°F (-20°C) last night but is 32°F (0°C) this morning, b) 7 inches (18 centimeters) of new snow fell overnight, c) southeasterly winds gusting to 20 mph (10 meters/second) are transporting some snow, d) the slope is leeward with a measured angle of 36°.

Within the bull's-eye exists the most useful or *meaningful* information with the highest degree of certainty in its message. Examples: a) recent avalanche activity on slopes with similar aspects and angles, b) the snow on small test slopes is fracturing when jumped on, c) very easy shear test results, and d) signs of significant wind-loading including hollow-sounding snow with a rippled wind slab texture and/or shooting cracks. Best yet, perhaps the slope you are concerned about avalanches while you are watching!

IN SEEKING INFORMATION,
GO FOR THE BULL'S-EYE!

IS THE TERRAIN CAPABLE OF PRODUCING AN AVALANCHE?

The term *avalanche path* defines the area in which an avalanche runs. A large avalanche path is generally divided into three parts. The *starting zone* is where the unstable snow or ice breaks loose and starts to slide. The *track* is the slope or channel down which snow moves at a fairly uniform speed. The *runout or deposition zone* is where the snow slows down and comes to rest. For large avalanches, the runout zone can include a powderblast zone that extends far beyond the area of snow deposition. *Powderblast* is a wave of displaced air containing a suspension of fine-grained snow particles that often precedes the debris of fast-moving avalanches, particularly dry slabs and ice avalanches.

Complex paths may contain multiple starting zones or extensive starting zones within the track area. Sometimes small starting zones such as stream banks or small steep slopes exist in the runout zone. In smaller

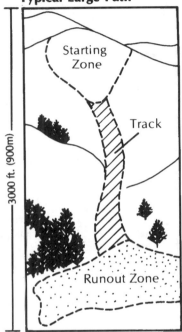

Typical Large Path

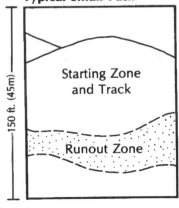

Typical Small Path

14

paths involving little vertical drop, the starting zone and track may be indistinguishable.

Keep in mind that any steep, snow-filled slope is a potential avalanche path given the right circumstances. Even creek banks less than 40 feet (12 meters) high have produced deadly avalanches.

Learning to recognize avalanche terrain is the critical starting point in the hazard evaluation process. Many people who have been caught in avalanches did not recognize the hazard until it was too late. A common mistake is to assume that avalanches occur only in large, obvious paths and to ignore the small terrain traps just beyond the parking lot. Another is to assume that it is safe to travel along the valley bottoms without considering the slopes above. The following factors influence

Although small, this avalanche path has all the necessary elements to be potentially deadly. It is steep, smooth and, before it released, leeward and loaded. The debris in the runout zone weighed over 2 million pounds (907,184 kg).

whether a given slope is capable of producing an avalanche and will help you recognize avalanche terrain.

SLOPE ANGLE

Slope angle is the most important terrain variable determining whether or not it is possible for a given slope to avalanche. **The underlying concept is that as the slope angle increases, so does the stress exerted on all of the boundary regions of the slab.**

Slab avalanches in cold snow are possible *only* within a certain range of slope angles, *generally* between 25° and 60°+. The word generally is highlighted because this range is variable and depends on a number of factors, including climate. Above roughly 60°, the stresses on the snowpack are so great that the snow tends to continually sluff off. On slope angles less than approximately 25°, the stresses on the snowpack are usually not great enough to cause the snow to slide. As previously described, slush flow avalanches which occur mostly at high latitudes commonly release on lower slope angles.

Most slab avalanches release on slopes with starting zone angles between 35° to 40°. Regionally, critical angles for slab failure are determined largely by snow climate and the nature of the instability. In cooler continental climates such as Colorado where the snowpack is often thin and weak, critical or "prime time" angles *tend* to be in the mid to high 30's. In warmer, maritime climates with deeper and sometimes stronger snowpacks, prime time angles typically range from the high 30's to the mid-40's. In studying numerous avalanches, it is striking how often the bed surface slope angle is measured at 37° and 38°.

It is important to know that your motion or body weight can trigger an avalanche even if you are on a low angle slope or on the flats as long as this terrain is connected to a slope with an angle of roughly 25° and instability exists. Usually there will be many clues indicating this kind of sensitive instability.

16

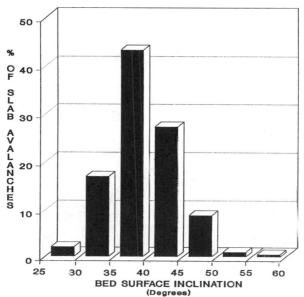

This chart, based upon 194 samples, shows the percentage of dry slab failures by bed surface slope angle. (Source: Perla, 1977, "Slab Avalanche Measurements," Canadian Geotechnical Journal, Volume 14, No. 2, National Research Council Canada.)

Continually ask yourself, "Is the slope steep enough to slide?" It is critical to judge slope angles correctly. The most reliable means is to *measure* them with an inexpensive inclinometer or slope meter which is built into some compasses. An inclinometer is an invaluable tool to always bring with you in the mountains. By putting numbers on the slope, that is, knowing exactly what the slope angles are, you will eliminate much of your uncertainty concerning whether or not the slope can avalanche. It is also helpful for categorizing the particular kind of instability on a given day. The slab depth, distribution, and structure as well as the type of weak layer will influence what slope angles the snow is likely to fail on. If you see recent fractures, measure the bed surface slope angles, if it is possible to do so safely, so that you can get a handle on the nature of the beast you are dealing with.

This avalanche initially failed on the steepest (49°) portion of the slope in the shadow. Then, as is common, it stepped down to a deeper weak layer and propagated across to the lower angle (30°) slope in the foreground of the above photo. This part of the 5 foot (1.5 m) fracture is shown in greater detail below.

SLOPE ASPECT (ORIENTATION)

Which direction is the slope facing relative to both recent winds and the sun? Subtle changes in slope aspect can greatly affect snow stability. Be suspicious of leeward, that is, wind-loaded slopes because the deposition of wind-transported snow increases the stress on the snowpack and enhances slab formation. You may find that the snow on a slope that is consistently wind-loaded throughout the winter is very homogenous and well-bonded but you need to check it out! Cornices also develop on leeward aspects.

The skier who was killed in this avalanche did not recognize the significance of recent wind-loading. Note that there is no snow on the windward side of the ridge. The snow on the leeward side was as hollow-sounding as a drum and with a ski pole, it was possible to push down through consolidated, fresh wind slab into weak, sugary snow. Note also the typically variable thickness of the slab along the flank.

Moderate warming by the sun can help strengthen and stabilize the snowpack. Intense, direct sun can have the opposite effect by weakening and lubricating the bonds between grains.

On shaded slopes, weak layers often persist or are more well-developed because of generally colder conditions and the absence of solar warming during much of the winter. Therefore, suspect instability on shadowed slopes.

The weak layer that lurked to help produce this slab avalanche did not exist on the ridge or other aspects that received more solar warming. In Alaska and other high latitude areas, most slopes (regardless of aspect) are essentially shadowed in early to mid-winter because of the low angle of incidence of the sun.

TERRAIN ROUGHNESS (ANCHORING)

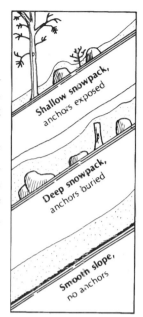

Boulders, trees, and ledges act as anchors and help hold the snow in place *until* the anchors themselves are buried. A grassy slope might avalanche with a total snow cover of only 1 foot (.3 meters) while a slope covered with large boulders might require deeper snow. Slopes with anchors are less likely to avalanche than open slopes, but the anchors (including trees) have to be too closely spaced together for a person to easily travel through to ensure that an avalanche cannot occur.

Anchors are commonly areas of stress concentration because the snow upslope of them is

The anchoring ability of a slope refers not only to the terrain roughness, but also to the old snow surface. How well do you think the next layer of snow will bond to these icy slopes, particularly if the storm begins at cold temperatures?

21

being held in place while the snow below or to the sides is being pulled downhill by gravity. For this reason, anchors can be starting points for initial failure to occur and fractures often run from tree to tree to rock. Furthermore, as discussed in the snowpack section, rocky protrusions and bushes can be "gardens" for the development of weak snow and thus, the snowpack is sometimes more easily triggered in these areas.

SLOPE SHAPE

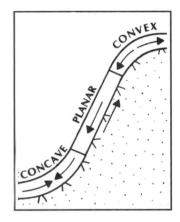

Avalanches can happen on any snow-covered slope steep enough to slide. On convex slopes, slabs are most likely to fracture just below the bulge where stresses are greatest. However, if the snow is highly unstable and sensitive, it is not uncommon for the fracture to break above the rollover. On broad, smooth (planar) slopes, avalanches can happen anywhere. Slabs often fracture below cliff bands. Small concave slopes can provide a certain amount of compressive support at the base of the hollow, thus inhibiting slab failure, particularly if the slopes are not very high (e.g., 15-30 feet or 4.5-9 meters). On larger concave slopes, there is not sufficient compressive support to be able to withstand the stresses associated with the steeper slopes above. The bottom line is that all concave slopes are capable of avalanching and it is often difficult to predict where the fracture will initiate.

Slope shape also influences the flow characteristics of an avalanche such as velocity and type of motion as well as the depth and distribution of debris. Beware of terrain traps, that is, steep slopes which end in v-shaped creek bottoms, cliffs, or ravines. Deposition in these areas tends to be deep and the consequences of entrapment are often serious. Slopes which run out onto alluvial fans or gentle, open slopes tend to produce shallower, but more widespread debris deposits.

Slabs often, but not always, fail just below a convexity. Note that the slope angle below the crown face pictured is 45° while the angle of the slope above the fracture is only 25°. It is not uncommon, however, for tender instabilities to break above the rollover or even to pull snow off of a flat ridge.

VEGETATION

Vegetation can provide evidence of both the frequency and magnitude of past avalanche occurrences and thus indicate potential avalanche terrain as well as the capability of a given path. Vegetative indicators include:

* ❄ swaths of open slope between forested or vegetated areas;
* ❄ trees which are bent, broken, or uprooted, "broomed" trees (i.e., previously broken but with new growth tops), and vegetation which is polished or "flagged" (i.e., missing branches on the up-hill side). Flagging can also indicate the flow height of the avalanches which have impacted the area;
* ❄ presence of "disaster species" such as alders, willows, dwarf birch, and cottonwoods;

23

❋ marked difference in height of trees (e.g., smaller spruce in the path, larger on the edges).

ELEVATION

Temperature, wind, and precipitation often vary significantly with elevation. Common differences are rain at lower elevations with snow at higher elevations or differences in precipitation amounts or wind speed with elevation. Generally, upper elevation areas are subjected to greater amounts of snowfall, stronger winds, and colder temperatures (except during periods of inversions). Never assume that conditions at one test site will reflect those at a different elevation.

This "flagged" tree, with broken branches on the uphill side, provides information concerning the frequency and flow heights of the avalanches causing the damage. (Photo by U.S. Forest Service)

PATH HISTORY

Every avalanche path has a history. It is not a question of *if* the path will produce an avalanche, but rather *when*, under what conditions, and how big. Learn about the path history of the area where you are travelling, not only by seeking clues at the site but also by talking with knowledgeable travellers, avalanche specialists, park rangers, and local people familiar with the area. Note, however, that many of the smaller paths or terrain traps most likely to catch travellers are often overlooked. In addition, be aware that as humans, our period of observation is very short in relation to the life of an avalanche path.

Path history may not always be evident, particularly in small paths or those above treeline. The group skiing near the shadow line in the photo above may not be aware of the runout potential of the nearby slope as shown in the photograph below.

* * * * *

If the answer to the question "Is the terrain capable of producing an avalanche?" is "yes," then you either need to go somewhere where the answer is "no" or confront the next question.

25

COULD THE SNOW SLIDE?

SNOWPACK LAYERING AND BONDING

The snowpack accumulates layer by layer with each new snow or wind event. These layers are then subject to changes in texture and strength throughout the winter. The changes help determine snow strength by influencing how well individual snow grains are bonded to each other both within a layer and between layers. Some layers are strong, others are weak. Strong layers tend to be made up of well-bonded, small, rounded grains. Weak layers are made up of poorly bonded or cohesionless grains. A thin weak layer or discontinuity (i.e., shear plane) can be created simply if one layer is poorly bonded to another.

Many combinations of strong and weak layers can exist within the snowpack. The structure of the snowpack varies greatly depending upon the particular season, location, and climate. Even on a small slope, the distribution and characteristics of snow layers may change within a few feet or meters, often due to subtle changes in slope aspect, inclination, and shape.

Do not be misled by the terms weak and strong. Strong does *not* necessarily mean stable. A strong layer is cohesive enough to fail initially as a slab. What is important is the *relative* cohesiveness of the layers. **Slab avalanche potential exists when relatively strong, cohesive snow overlies weaker snow or is not bonded well to the underlying layer.**

A common misconception is to assume that cohesive snow is snow that you can pick up in chunks. Cohesive snow can be soft, powdery snow that you almost need a snorkel to travel through or can be very hard, wind-deposited snow that it is difficult to kick toeholds into. **Snow that is cohesive enough to propagate a fracture is potential slab material, regardless of hardness.**

26

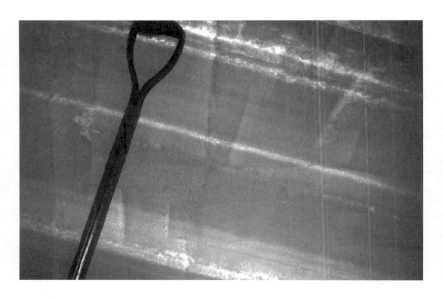

Not only is the snowpack layered, but the strength, thickness and distributuon of these layers changes over time. Above, note the stronger (darker) and weaker (lighter) layers evident in a thin wall backlit by the sun. Similar shear planes are evident in some fracture lines such as the one below.

Snow metamorphism is the name given to describe the changes in structure that take place over time within the layers of the snowpack. There are several types of snow metamorphism. Each occurs under a different set of conditions and as discussed, each affects the strength of the snowpack. As conditions change, the dominant type of metamorphism in a given layer may change. Also importantly, different types of metamorphism may be occurring in various layers of the snowpack at the same time.

The rate of change, that is, the speed at which any type of metamorphism occurs, depends on the average snowpack temperature. The warmer the temperature, the faster metamorphism takes place. The colder the temperature, the slower the rate of change. This is called the "Betty Crocker principle", that is, you can bake a cake at 200°F (93°C) but it will cook much faster at 400°F (204°C). In fact, all changes within the snowpack happen faster when it is warmer. For this reason, instabilities within the snowpack tend to be more shortlived at warmer temperatures and more persistent at colder temperatures.

Whether you remember the different types of metamorphism or can definitively identify different types of snow grains is unimportant. What is critical is that you are able to recognize relatively strong and weak layers in the field. However, if you do learn something about the conditions that produce different kinds of layers (i.e., potential slabs, weak layers, and bed or sliding surfaces), you will be better able to anticipate the stability of the snowpack before you even reach the trailhead. If you want to learn more about snow metamorphism, read on. If not, skip to: Recipe for a Slab Avalanche.

MORE ABOUT SNOW METAMORPHISM

The two types of metamorphism which take place in cold, dry snow have been known in recent years as equitemperature (ET) and temperature gradient (TG). The international terminology was revamped in 1990 and two parallel classifications were developed to describe metamorphic types either by the process that occurs or by the morphology (shape and structure) of the resulting grains. ET snow is now called equilibrium form or more simply, rounded grains (rounds). TG snow is called kinetic growth form or faceted grains (facets). The presence or absence of a significant temperature gradient, that is, a difference in temperature across a given distance, determines whether rounded or faceted grains develop within a given layer. The third type of metamorphism is known either as melt-freeze (MF) or wet grains.

Rounded grains develop when the temperature in a layer or between layers is fairly uniform, that is, there is no significant temperature gradient. While individual grains become smaller and rounder, bonds or necks between grains are developed. This bonding process is known

If you looked at a thin section of this wind slab under a hand lens, you would see fine, rounded grains as shown in the inset. Note the "necks" or bonds between grains.

as sintering and increases the strength of a layer. Thus, the equilibrium form process produces fine, rounded, well-bonded grains and the result is a relatively strong layer, with moderate to high density. Remember not to confuse the terms strong and stable. Strong snow makes good slab material because it is cohesive enough to be able to propagate a fracture.

Favorable conditions or habitat for the development of rounded grains are cloudy, mild weather or a thick snowpack. Every metamorphic process has an early, intermediate, and advanced stage. The more advanced the equilibrium form process, the smaller, rounder, and better bonded the grains will be.

Faceted grains develop when a significant temperature gradient exists within or between layers. In most areas, the temperature at the ground/snow interface is warmer than the air temperature. The shallower the snowpack, the greater the temperature gradient within the snowpack. Deep snowpacks tend to dampen this difference by adding many layers of insulation between the relatively warm ground and cold air. A significant gradient in a snowpack where the average temperature is close to 0°C or 32°F is 1°C per 10 centimeters (1.8°F per 4 inches). This is also equal to 10°C per meter or 18°F per 3.3 feet. In very cold areas such as the Canadian Rockies or interior Alaska, where the average snowpack temperature is usually much colder than 0°C, it takes more of a gradient to drive the kinetic growth form process.

The trend of the kinetic growth form process is to produce large, angular grains which are poorly bonded and weak, especially in shear. The longer the gradient exists and the process continues, the larger, more faceted, and more persistent the grains. Because faceted grains have much the same consistency as sugar, they are sometimes referred to as sugar snow. In Canada, they are called "squares." Advanced faceted grains are also known as depth hoar. Faceted snow is often the layer that collapses and goes "whumph" as you travel. It is particularly sensitive as a weak layer when subjected to significant loading of new or wind-transported snow.

There is a tendency to focus on the large, obvious depth hoar which is at the bottom of many snowpacks but it is important to recognize that faceted grains can form at any level of the snowpack and can be a significant weak layer at *any* stage of development. One scenario for developing faceted grains in the upper part of a deep snowpack is to have several inches of new snow followed by a prolonged period of cold, clear weather. Surface hoar, explained later in this section, may develop along the snow surface but the rest of the layer, with cold temperatures near the snow/air interface and relatively warm snow underneath, will be exposed to a temperature gradient and begin to develop faceted grains. If the process does not continue for long, the grains may not have time to develop obvious cupped facets. Instead, they will just be slightly uncohesive and angular and yet could be very tender when the next load is deposited.

Favorable conditions for the development of faceted grains are cold weather and/or a thin snowpack. Also, because temperature gradients are likely to develop on either side of ice crusts or very dense layers, these interfaces are likely habitats for faceted grains. In addition, these grains need relatively low density (high porosity) snow in order to have room to grow. Perhaps you have had the unexpected treat of suddenly plunging deep into the snowpack when you are near rocks, tree wells, or bushes. Chances are you've just found sugar snow. These are likely spots for faceted grains to develop because they have plenty of open or pore space around them and because they sometimes have greater temperature gradients. If, however, a temperature gradient is introduced within a dense, hard wind slab made up of small, rounded grains, the kinetic growth form process will take over as the driving type of metamorphism but it is unlikely that any substantial change in structure will occur because there is not enough pore space.

Faceted grains, in any stage of development, can be a potential weak layer although there is a tendency to focus on the large, cupped, advanced facets or depth hoar crystals shown above. In the 14 inch (36 cm) fracture below, the slab was made up of early facets, the weak layer of intermediate facets, and the bed surface of advanced facets. What was important was that the slab was relatively cohesive compared to the underlying snow. The entire snowpack was only knee deep and was so soft that a boot easily penetrated to the gound. As cold weather and the resulting temperature gradient persisted, the entire snowpack developed into advanced facets. Though some loose snow slides occurred, there were no further slab avalanches until the next storm load produced widespread activity. (Above photo by Bill Glude)

As mentioned, advanced faceted grains will persist as an obvious discontinuity long after the temperature gradient has dissipated and the equilibrium form process has taken over as the type of metamorphism in the layer (thus causing the grains to round somewhat). The reason why "bootpacking" steep slopes is a common practice at some ski areas is to densify the snow, inhibiting the growth of faceted grains and thereby preventing the development of a weak layer which could prove to be a season-long problem.

One way to completely eliminate depth hoar as a potential weak layer is to have the slope avalanche on the faceted grains at the ground and then have a series of storms quickly deposit heavy amounts of snow. This will essentially insulate the relatively warm ground from the cooler air and may prevent these layers from developing faceted grains. Another is for heavy rain to percolate into the depth hoar and then have the entire layer refreeze. Often, however, advanced faceted grains will exist in the snowpack throughout the winter. These grains, while weak in shear, can be very strong in compression. Failure may or may not occur depending on whether stress is increased, incrementally or at once, to critical levels. Avalanches to the ground and whumphing (collapsing) noises are bull's-eye clues that the depth hoar is sensitive!

Melt-freeze metamorphism occurs during mid-winter thaws or in the spring, when meltwater or rain enters the snowpack and the snowpack temperature reaches 0°C (32°F). The trend is toward the production of coarse, rounded grains and with repeated cycles of melting and refreezing, these grains become larger and larger. Melt-freeze or wet grains are also known as corn snow. In the freeze phase, these grains are well-bonded and strong. The resulting ice crusts can, however, make good potential bed surfaces for slabs formed on top of them. In the melt phase, wet grains weaken rapidly and are lubricated by the presence of free water. This is why timing is so critical in the spring near steep slopes that are being subjected to warming.

Melt freeze or wet grains such as those above are formed after repeated cycles of melting and refreezing. Rain can accelerate this process and produce wet slab avalanches like the one below.

There are other important weak layers. *Surface hoar* or hoar frost, the wintertime equivalent of summertime dew, is formed at the snow surface during cold, clear weather. Surface hoar crystals are loose, feath-

Surface hoar, though delicate in structure, can persist as a potentially unstable shear plane for weeks or months. Note that the weak layer of surface hoar is still evident even after it was overrun by the shallow wind slab pictured. The skier who triggered this slide missed several key clues: a long, cold, clear period followed by new snow and little wind until the end of the storm (this is significant because the surface hoar was buried rather than being destroyed by rain or wind), steep slope angle, and fresh wind slab texture on this lee slope. The large surface hoar crystals in the inset photograph are roughly a half inch (1.3 cm) wide.

ery, and poorly bonded. Surface hoar is a potentially deadly weak layer once buried because it persists for a long period of time, can form a thin shear plane that is difficult to detect if you are not looking for it, and can produce long-running "zipper" fractures. However, the conditions leading up to the problem can be quite obvious. For example, picture yourself bemoaning the lack of recent snowfall and travelling along through delightful, "tinkly-sounding" snow. The next day there is a large dump of new snow. Rather than jumping onto the slopes with "recreation eyeballs", head out into the mountains with "avalanche eyeballs", anticipating that the buried surface hoar might be a serious problem.

Another significant weak layer is *unmetamorphosed new snow*. This is snow that may have fallen during a cool or windless period of a storm and then had denser, heavier snow deposited on top of it. Still another is *graupel*, a type of precipitation. These rounded, iced pellets often roll downslope and collect in depressions or at the bottom of cliff bands, thus forming an area that may be more sensitive once the next load is deposited.

Rounded grains often make up slabs while faceted grains can form classic weak layers. However, slab avalanches have occurred in which the slabs were composed of early faceted grains, the weak layer of intermediate faceted grains, and the bed surface of advanced faceted grains or depth hoar. On the other hand, if the entire snowpack is composed of a homogenous layer of faceted snow (i.e., equally uncohesive, with no structural discontinuities), there is little or no potential for slab failure under most circumstances although loose snow releases may occur. Any layer can be a bed surface, even very soft, powdery snow, so it is best to focus attention on potential slabs and weak layers. Remember that what is critical in terms of snow stability is the relative cohesiveness of the layers and how well the layers are bonded to each other.

SNOW METAMORPHISM SUMMARY

● *ROUNDS/EQUILIBRIUM FORM*
    CONDITIONS
    - Lack of significant temperature gradient
    - Cloudy, warm
    -Thick snowpack
    SIGNIFICANCE
    Strong (strong does not necessarily equal stable), well-
        bonded layer, cohesive slab material

☐ *FACETS/KINETIC GROWTH FORM*
    CONDITIONS
    - Significant temperature gradient
    - Shallow snowpack
    - Cold, weather
    - Near crusts
    - On shadowed aspects
    - Lower density, more porous snow
    - Near rocks, trees
    SIGNIFICANCE
    Weak, poorly bonded layer (early, intermediate, &
        advanced stages of development), collapsible, per-
        sistent

○ *WET GRAINS/MELT-FREEZE*
    CONDITIONS
    - Melting/freezing temperatures
    - Rain or warm weather
    SIGNIFICANCE
    Freeze = strong (but crust often makes good future
    sliding surface)
    Melt = weak (rapid weakening, free water lubrication)

TYPICAL UNSTABLE SNOW STRUCTURES
IN DRY SNOW*

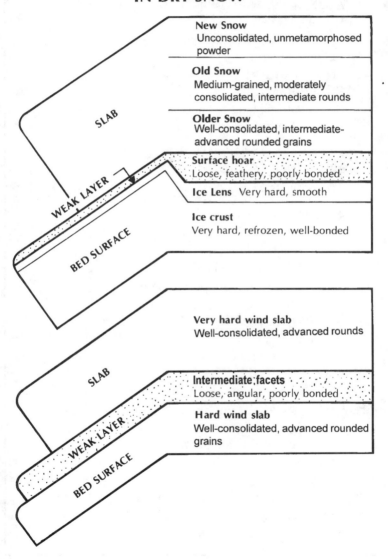

New Snow
Unconsolidated, unmetamorphosed powder

Old Snow
Medium-grained, moderately consolidated, intermediate rounds

Older Snow
Well-consolidated, intermediate-advanced rounded grains

Surface hoar
Loose, feathery, poorly bonded

Ice Lens Very hard, smooth

Ice crust
Very hard, refrozen, well-bonded

SLAB

WEAK LAYER

BED SURFACE

Very hard wind slab
Well-consolidated, advanced rounds

Intermediate facets
Loose, angular, poorly bonded

Hard wind slab
Well-consolidated, advanced rounded grains

SLAB

WEAK LAYER

BED SURFACE

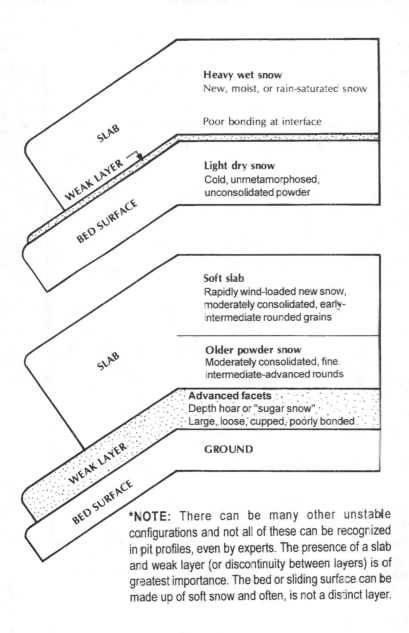

Heavy wet snow
New, moist, or rain-saturated snow

Poor bonding at interface

Light dry snow
Cold, unmetamorphosed, unconsolidated powder

SLAB

WEAK LAYER

BED SURFACE

Soft slab
Rapidly wind-loaded new snow, moderately consolidated, early-intermediate rounded grains

Older powder snow
Moderately consolidated, fine, intermediate-advanced rounds

Advanced facets
Depth hoar or "sugar snow". Large, loose, cupped, poorly bonded

GROUND

SLAB

WEAK LAYER

BED SURFACE

*NOTE: There can be many other unstable configurations and not all of these can be recognized in pit profiles, even by experts. The presence of a slab and weak layer (or discontinuity between layers) is of greatest importance. The bed or sliding surface can be made up of soft snow and often, is not a distinct layer.

39

RECIPE FOR A SLAB AVALANCHE

If you have a slab, a weak layer, and maybe even an obvious bed surface, do you have all the ingredients necessary for a slab avalanche? The answer is an emphatic NO! This is important to remember if you want to keep your paranoia factor down to a reasonable level because in almost every snowpack, every winter, you will see strong and weak layers.

In a stable snowpack, the strength of the snow is greater than the stress exerted on it. For an avalanche to occur, something must *upset* this balance so that the stress on, or within, the snowpack becomes equal to or greater than its strength. The balance can be tipped either by: 1) an increase in stress, 2) a decrease in strength, or 3) a combination of both.

In the first case, imagine a strong man on whose shoulders we place a 100 pound (45 kilo) sack. If we want to get the man to collapse and fail, we merely have to pile more sacks on him until he can no longer hold them. This is similar to a snowpack that fails with the additional stress of new snow loading, wind-transported snow, or the weight of an unsuspecting mountain traveller.

In the second case, we can illustrate failure by loading a 100 pound (45 kilo) sack on the shoulders of the same strong man but instead of adding more load, we ask him to hold the weight for as long as he can. How long he lasts depends on his strength but given enough time, eventually he will collapse to the floor. This is similar to weakening of the snowpack through internal changes.

INGREDIENTS FOR A SLAB AVALANCHE

SUITABLY STEEP TERRAIN

+

UNSTABLE SNOW STRUCTURE

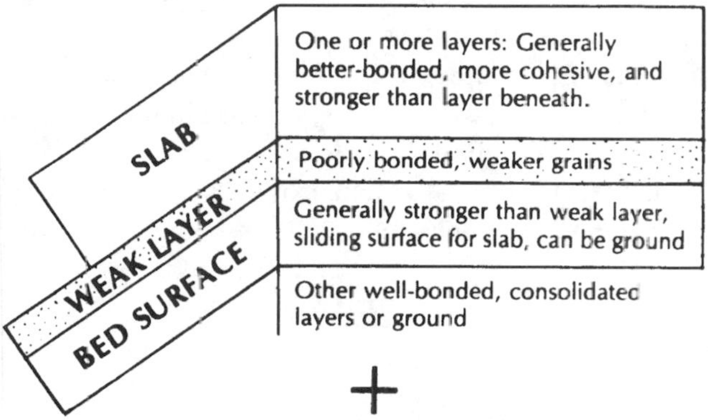

SLAB	One or more layers: Generally better-bonded, more cohesive, and stronger than layer beneath.
WEAK LAYER	Poorly bonded, weaker grains
BED SURFACE	Generally stronger than weak layer, sliding surface for slab, can be ground
	Other well-bonded, consolidated layers or ground

+

CRITICAL BALANCE BETWEEN STRESS/STRENGTH (i.e., stored elastic energy)

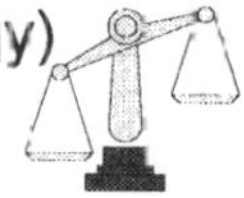

+

SOMETHING TO TIP THE BALANCE

(LIKELY TRIGGERS)

= **AVALANCHE**

The snowpack can only adjust to a certain amount of stress and only at a certain rate of speed. A condition of *instability* exists when the stress exerted upon the snowpack is almost equal to the strength of the snowpack. **When stress equals or exceeds strength, failure occurs.** This concept of a stress/strength relationship applies to all of the slab boundaries. Failure at one slab boundary increases the stress at the other slab boundaries and can result in failure of the entire slope.

As previously described, the bed surface is the most important slab boundary because it has the greatest surface area. Most slab avalanches appear to be initiated by a failure in shear at the interface between the slab and the bed surface (see below). Almost simultaneously, this shear failure may cause a failure in tension in the area of the fracture line, in shear and tension along the flanks of the slab, and in compression and shear along the stauchwall or bottom boundary of the slab.

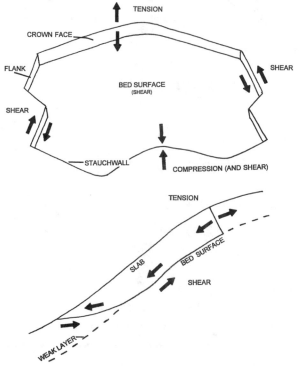

Occasionally, a shear failure will take place along the bed surface (you may or may not hear a whumph) but the slope will not avalanche. This is usually because the slope is not steep enough to produce failure at the other slab boundaries. At times, however, these shear failures may propagate a considerable distance and cause slab failure where slope angles are steep enough to provide sufficient stress.

It is critical to note that stress and strength are not evenly distributed across a slope due to terrain and snowpack irregularities. It is common to have tender or weak spots on a slope, that is, areas where the snowpack is weaker or the stress on the snowpack is greater.

Tender spots can be thought of as buttons where a slope can be more easily triggered. Some call these "sweet spots" but considering the potential consequences, this terminology is misleading--"sour spots" may be more appropriate. You need to be suspicious of steep areas where the snowpack is shallow or near rocks, bushes and trees, where the development of weak layers of faceted snow is favored and avalanches often run to the ground. Likely tender spots can also be where there is a terrain break such as a rollover or where the slope steepens. Sometimes you will be able to detect tender spots after an avalanche has already run. Study these carefully as this will help you develop good "x-ray avalanche eyeballs" for snow-covered slopes. Fractures commonly start in these areas and propagate into areas of stronger, often deeper, snow.

It is also important to understand that the stability of the snowpack is relative to the force applied to it. For example, a slope with a hairtrigger balance between stress and strength might be triggered by a skier just approaching the edge of it. If the snowpack on the same slope is just a bit stronger (that is, the stress/strength balance is a little less critical), it might require two snowmachiners, or one skier falling, or one snowboarder jumping off a cornice, or one climber crossing over a tender spot to trigger an avalanche. There have been avalanche accidents in which snowmachiners have played highmark on a slope for an hour, with numerous runs, before the slope failed.

Imagine this slope before it avalanched. Using your "avalanche eyeballs," try to identify the critical factors that might make this slope more susceptible to failure. A few answers: it is steep (38°-42°), smooth/poorly anchored, leeward, newly loaded, and shadowed. It also has two convex curvatures. The likely tender spot is the mid-slope breakover where the angle not only steepens but the development of weak, faceted snow also may have been encouraged amid the rocks and bushes.

It is also possible to have a slope that is so stable that hundreds of people can ski it, fall on it, or even drive a herd of elephants across it without triggering an avalanche. If you are determined to make that slope avalanche, you will need to increase the stress exerted on the snowpack to the point at which it equals the snowpack's tremendous strength. Maybe 10,000 elephants will do it, but at this point it is becoming a bit academic and it would be more fun to go skiing, snowmobiling, snowboarding, or whatever.

FIELD TESTS AND OBSERVATIONS

Snow stability evaluation, the process of determining if the snowpack is capable of avalanching, is just a fancy name for "hammering" on the snowpack to see how it will respond. It is an ongoing process which continues during every

The weight of a skier or a snowmachine with a rider or the impact of a falling person is often all that is required to trigger an unstable snowpack. In this case, the angle of the slope was too gentle to produce an avalanche when this skier "augered in" even though the same instability that produced the avalanche in the background existed on this slope.

45

step of a climb, each turn of a ski, but it does not have to take a lot of time. Remember to start by formulating an opinion about the stability of the snow before you even head outside. This will help you identify what you know and don't know about what has been happening in the mountains. Be willing to change your opinion based upon new information.

Remove your blinders by getting off the broken trail frequently. Look, listen, and feel for clues (or lack of clues) to instability. There are almost always clues letting you know how sensitive the snowpack is. It is your job not to ignore them.

BULL'S-EYE CLUES TO INSTABILITY INCLUDE:

"NATURE'S BILLBOARDS"	THE MESSAGE
Recent Avalanche Activity on Similar Slopes	There is no clue more emphatic in its message about avalanche potential than evidence of recent avalanche activity. Avoid slopes of similar angles, aspects, and elevations which have not yet released.
Whumphing Noises	Whumphs are the sounds made when a weak layer (commonly faceted grains but also surface hoar, unmetamorphosed new snow, and others) collapses within the snowpack. Instability exists and nature is literally scream-

ing in your ear! Measure your slope angles carefully. Avoid travelling on slopes steep enough to slide or in runout zones where you could trigger the slopes above you. Whumphs, particularly loud, distinct ones, often indicate the type of instability that can propagate over a distance. Sometimes after a storm, you will hear whumphing noises on the flats, but not on steeper slopes which may have already collapsed because of the additional stress of slope angle. Remain very distrustful of avalanche terrain until you understand the instability you are dealing with. Note: Some people use the term "settling" instead of collapsing or whumphing. We would like to discourage use of this term as it is too easily confused with the very different settlement process which strengthens the snowpack.

Shooting Cracks

Cracks shooting out in the snow around you indicate the spontaneous release of stored elastic energy. In other words, they are a "red flag" that the snow is cohesive enough to propagate fractures and are a major clue to instability. The longer the cracks, the more tender the instability. Shallow, localized cracking within a narrow radius of a few feet around you usually represents less of a threat but still warrants checking out as it is an indicator that the surface layer is acting differently than the layer underneath. It may just be a breakable layer like a crust or it may be a thin slab. Pay attention to the depth and distribution of the slab. A slab that is a few inches thick in one spot may be over a foot thick just a short distance across the slope.

Recent Wind-Loading

Evidence of deposition of wind-transported snow includes smooth "pillows", cornices, and drift patterns on the snow surface and around obstacles. Such wind-loading increases the stress exerted on the snowpack and greatly enhances slab formation.

Snow texture patterns are often a more reliable indicator of recent wind direction than cornices which can build on both sides of a ridge in response to winds from opposite directions. These patterns tell a story of how the snow has been distributed and acted upon by the wind--learn to read them! Constantly scanning ahead for changes in these patterns could prevent you from stumbling onto a wind slab. When deposition has occurred, drift tails point the way the wind is blowing, much like an arrow from a drawn bow.

Tails and rippled patterns will extend from the leeward side of rocks, trees, or across slopes. Erosion causes the snow surface to be undercut on the windward side, with the undercut tail pointing into the wind.

If you see wind pluming (blowing snow) or flat, lenticular clouds indicating strong winds aloft, ask yourself how much snow is available for transport, how much loading is occurring, which slopes are being loaded, and at what rate. Suspect instability on wind-loaded or lee slopes. If you see evidence of snow erosion by wind, think about where the windblown snow was deposited.

Hollow Sounds

These hollow, sometimes drum-like sounds indicate unstable layering, that is, a less consolidated, potentially weak layer is overcapped by a denser layer. Investigate!

These are just some of Nature's clues. **You do not have to see recent avalanches, hear whumphing noises, or have shooting cracks to get caught in an avalanche.** You might only know that there was a recent dump of snow or that the wind was howling. You absolutely will have some combination of clues available to you. Seek them out and listen to their message!

Evidence of recent avalanche activity is the best clue of all regarding current snow stability. On what angles, aspects, and at what elevations are the slides releasing? How deep or extensive are they? How far are they running? Is there a pattern? Note that cornice breaks, slab avalanches, and loose snow slides are all visible in this photograph.

This shooting crack is indisputable evidence that the snow is storing elastic energy and is capable of propagating fractures. Long-running, deep cracks like this one indicate especially sensitive snow. Even without such obvious cracking, the rippled snow surface texture is a clue that the wind has been acting on the snow and demands that you know something about how well the layers are bonded. If you miss all of these clues, you might still pick up on the hollow-sounding snow indicating that the wind slab is underlain by less dense, weaker snow. Do not ignore the message.

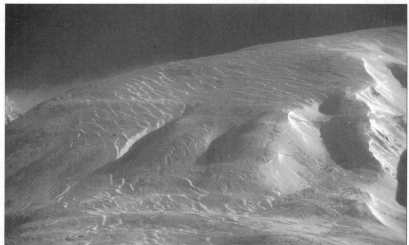

Always pay attention to surface texture patterns as indicators of where wind slabs may lurk. When wind deposition occurs, drift tails point the way the wind is blowing. Note that multiple clues -- pluming off the ridge, upslope drift tails, cornices, and avalanche activity -- all show that the wind has been blowing from left to right.

When wind erodes snow, it undercuts it on the windward side. This photo shows an erosional feature; thus the wind was blowing from right to left. Where did the windblown snow go? Be suspicious of loading on the next leeward rollover.

MORE ON STABILITY EVALUATION

Often, no single field test or observation will tell all. You must piece together the story the snowpack is trying to tell. You will usually find that the various pieces of information back each other up and tell the same story.

Approach small but steep hills from the top and jump on them to see how they respond. Depending on the instability, you can sometimes get very useful feedback from a slope that is only a few feet high. If you are switchbacking uphill on skis and have just turned a corner, jump just below your uphill ski track and see if you can get a "piece of the pie" to break into blocks, indicating that the snow may be cohesive enough to propagate a fracture.

Somewhere along the line, backcountry travellers have been made to feel that they have to dig a snowpit to evaluate snow stability. It is often possible to safely travel for many days, responsibly evaluating snow stability by integrating bull's-eye data, *without* digging a snowpit. A snowpit is just one piece of information, the quality of which depends greatly on where you choose to dig and how you conduct your tests. Pits can be misleading because snow structure and stability can vary greatly across any given slope with areas of weaker and stronger snow. A graphic example of this are all the variations in surface snow that we are accustomed to seeing as we travel--breakable crust in one spot, nice powder in another. These will become variations in layering once buried.

Digging a pit is one way of helping to eliminate uncertainty about the layering and bonding of the snowpack at a particular location. It can be especially helpful when travelling in new territory where you are unfamiliar with the season's snow and weather history. It does not have to take a lot of time. Indeed, it is usually far more useful to quickly integrate data (i.e., observations, clues, and/or snowpit tests) from a number of locations rather than spend an inordinate amount of time evaluating snowpit information from one spot.

Bull's-eye snow stability questions:
* ❋ *Is there a slab?*
* ❋ *If so, what is its depth and distribution?*
* ❋ *How well is it bonded to the layers beneath?*
* ❋ *How much force will it take to make the slab fail?*

Some ways to help get the information you need to answer these questions are shown on the following pages.

Ski Pole Test

This test takes only seconds and should be done often as you travel. Holding your ski pole at a right angle to the snow surface, gently push the handle end into the snowpack. Feel the relative hardness and the thickness of the layers. Be alert for well-consolidated layers that feel harder than underlying soft, weaker layers. This is also a way to keep track of the depth and distribution of potential slabs. Probe in several different spots.

Sometimes you may want to widen the hole with your pole using circular motions. Reach into the hole and, with your fingers, feel how hard or soft each layer is. If you like, pull out some grains and examine their structure.

One serious limitation of the ski pole test is that sometimes the weak layers are too thin to detect by this method. Another is that it does not tell you how well the layers are actually bonded to each other, except in cases of extreme instability resulting from gross discontinuities.

Snowpit Tests
(10-20 minutes)

Choose a spot with conditions similar to those you are trying to evaluate. In other words, select a site that has roughly the same elevation, snow conditions, slope angle (at least 30° if possible and preferably, a little steeper), and aspect as the slope you are concerned about. Probe the area to help locate a representative spot. If you detect areas where the snowpack is relatively thick and others where it is thin, you may want to check both. Fractures often initiate in thinner, weaker spots and then rip across into deeper snow. If there are several people in your group, have each person dig a quick pit in different places on the slope and then compare results. Balance safety with realism. Never conduct the following tests in a location where you might trigger a slide with serious consequences to yourself or others.

Now dig a pit 4-5 feet (1.25-1.5 meters) deep and wide enough for you to work in (approximately 4 feet or 1.25 meters). As you shovel, pay attention to changes in snow texture indicating weak and strong layers. Be careful not to disturb the snow surface surrounding the uphill portion of the pit. With your shovel, smooth off the uphill pit wall and adjacent, ideally shaded, side wall. These walls are where your tests will be conducted. It is important that they be smooth and vertical and that the snow above the uphill wall be untrampled.

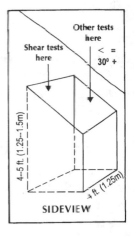

Most human-triggered slab releases occur within a depth of 4-5 feet (1.25-1.5 meters). It is not usually necessary to dig to the ground although it is a good idea to probe through the floor of the pit to check for obvious weak layers. If you know that a storm just deposited more than 5 feet of snow, especially if the new load came in on top of a sensitive layer like surface hoar, then dig deeper. The problem is that

55

the deeper you dig, the more difficult it is to interpret your results. If you suspect deep slab instability, it is usually best to avoid the slope.

Identifying Layers:

Stratigraphy Test

Using a whisk broom, paint brush, hat, or mitten, lightly brush the side wall of the pit with uniform strokes parallel to the snow surface. This will quickly transform the wall from a plain white surface into a layered mosaic of snow history. The layers of the snowpack will be revealed in a series of ridges and valleys.

The raised or ridged surfaces indicate the harder, stronger layers that may be possible slabs or sliding surfaces. The indented surfaces reveal softer, weaker layers.

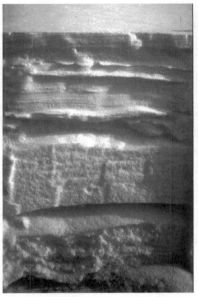

After brushing, strong and weak layers are quite evident in this side wall of this snowpit.

Resistance Test

Insert a credit card, saw, or any straight edge into the top of the side wall. Run the card down the wall, feeling the relative resistance of the layers and noting the boundaries of hard and soft layers. In helping to identify potential slab and weak layers, this test can help corroborate and expand upon the information gained from the stratigraphy test.

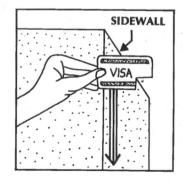

Hardness Test

Test the relative hardness of each layer by gently pushing your hand or fingers into the pit wall, applying about 10 pounds (4.5 kilograms) of pressure. One layer might be so soft that you can easily push your whole fist into it while another might require a knife to penetrate it. Layer hardness can be classified as fist (very soft), 4-finger (soft), 1-finger (medium), pencil (hard), or knife (very hard). An example of a potentially unstable slab configuration would

Very Soft	Fist (F)	
Soft	Four fingers (4F)	
Medium	One finger (1F)	
Hard	Pencil (P)	
Very Hard	Knife (K)	

Note: Test usually done with a gloved hand.

be a cohesive 1-finger hard layer resting on top of a less cohesive fist hard layer. This, in turn, could be underlain by a harder bed (sliding) surface with a hardness ranging anywhere from 4-finger to knife. As discussed, however, the bed surface does not have to be hard. Also, sometimes potential shear planes are too thin to be detected by your hand. You can just run your thumbs down the wall at roughly 2 inch (5 centimeter) intervals, pushing them in with equal force.

Remember that the strength of a layer is determined by how well the grains within it are bonded to each other. While strong layers are often hard and weak layers are often soft, note that this is not always the case. New powder snow can form cohesive slabs despite the fact that it might only be fist hard.

Testing Layer Bonding:

The tests just described yield a good visual representation of strong and weak layers, but still do not indicate how well the layers are bonded and how much force it will take to make them fail. To check this, you *must* conduct the shovel shear, ski shear, rutschblock, banzai jump test, or some combination of them. Such tests are critical because often they will reveal a previously undetected but serious weakness in the snowpack created by poor bonding between layers or a very thin, weak layer.

To understand the results of the following shear tests, it is important to remember that stability is relative to the amount and rate of stress exerted on the snowpack. By applying increasing degrees of force, we are able to gain a relative feel for the shear strength or bonding of the layers within the sample and relate this, along with other information, to the stability of the snowpack in a broader geographic area.

These tests require years of practice in the field to master. Their results are often misunderstood or misinterpreted, by experts as well as novices. We encourage you to experiment with these and other tests which have been developed and see which ones give you the best feel for the snowpack's reponse to stress.

Shovel/Ski Shear Test

Isolate a column in the uphill pit wall by cutting away the sides with a snow saw and/or shovel. The width of this column as well as the depth cut into the pit wall should be approximately 11 inches (28 centimeters), slightly wider than most small grain scoop shovels. Be sure the column is both vertical and smooth. If your column is leaning or uneven, your test results may be biased (i.e., garbage in, garbage out).

Cut the back of the column where it connects to the pit wall by sawing downward with a saw or string. The reason for cutting the back is so that you can test just the shear strength of the snow. In some depth hoar snowpacks, you may be unable to isolate a column without it collapsing. If you have tried several times and failed, build another column and as a last resort, shear it without unhinging the back wall. Whenever possible, however, cut the back wall of all of your test blocks.

Now, slowly insert your shovel or ski (tip up and binding facing upslope) at the back of the column and pull gently forward. A ski seems to yield better results than a shovel, except in very soft snow with surface instability, because it applies pressure more uniformly to the column.

Slab layers will usually shear off along a clean plane. An uneven surface may indicate that the block has been pried off. The ease *and* energy with which slab layers break is an indicator of how poorly the layers are bonded. If you barely touch the shovel or ski to the column and a layer shears off and almost jumps forward as if it is spring-loaded, the snowpack is tender, with very poor layer bonding, and likely to fail. On the other hand, a column that has to be hammered and levered loose indicates a fairly stable, well-bonded snowpack.

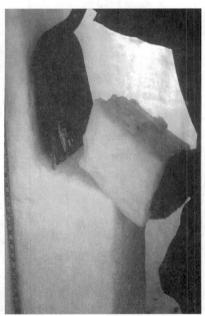

Two methods of detecting potential shear planes: the shovel shear test (on the left) and the ski shear test (on the right). Note that each tester has a hand positioned to catch the block as it slides forward so that the weak layer underneath can be identified.

The ease with which a column shears is rated as very easy, easy, moderate, hard, or very hard. Generally, very easy and easy shears are considered indicators of unstable snow while moderate, hard, and very hard shears reflect varying degrees of a stable snowpack. But again, stability is relative to the amount and rate of stress exerted on the snowpack. A moderate shear on a 30° slope might be an easy shear on a 45° slope because the snow on the steeper slope is subjected to greater stress. Likewise, a slope that may be safe for two skiers may release when a third person enters.

A *major* limitation of this test is that you are applying force to a very small column and trying to generalize the results. The test is easily biased by how the column is constructed and force is applied. It is a good idea to shear several columns and compare results.

Rutschblock (Shear Block) Test

This test is generally favored by avalanche professionals over the shovel or ski shear because it tests a larger area and gives you a feel for how sensitive the snowpack is to your weight. Excavate the test site as indicated in the diagram, being careful not to disturb the area surrounding the shear block. Make sure the walls are even and plumb

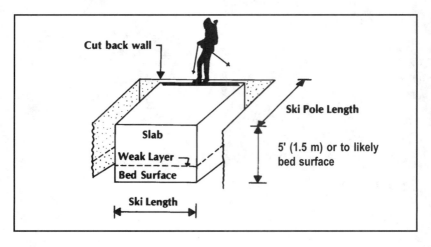

Cut back wall

Slab

Weak Layer

Bed Surface

Ski Length

Ski Pole Length

5' (1.5 m) or to likely bed surface

(vertical) before cutting the uphill wall with a snow saw, string, or ski. You are now ready. To save time, you can cut the sides of the block with a ski or snow saw rather than trenching. The disadvantage of this is that it is more difficult to be sure that you have completely isolated the rutschblock.

With skis on, carefully approach the shear block from above and step gently onto the block. Once standing parallel to the cut on the downhill side, flex your knees without lifting your heels in an attempt to apply light pressure to the shear block. If the slab doesn't fail, jump and land in the same compacted spot. Gradually increase the force of your jumps. After repeated jumps, change your landing spot so that you are now landing almost mid-block. You might now remove your skis, par-

The rutschblock test is an excellent way to test the snow's shear strength in response to the weight of a person. In the test shown, a 14 inch (36 cm) deep slab failed on only a 30° slope as soon as the tester stepped onto the block, thus indicating the likelihood of very unstable conditions.

ticularly if you are dealing with a hard or deep slab, and jump several last times.

WHAT DO THE SHEAR BLOCK TEST RESULTS MEAN?	
Level of Activity (Force)	*Degree of Stability*
1. Fails while excavating test site	Extremely unstable
2. Fails while approaching or gently stepping onto block	Extremely unstable
3. Fails while flexing knees	Extremely unstable
4. Fails with one jump (with skis on)	Unstable
5. Fails with two jumps (with skis on, same compacted spot)	Potentially unstable/ marginally stable
6. Fails after repeated hard jumps (with or without skis)	Relatively stable
7. Doesn't fail after repeated hard jumps (with skis off)	Stable or very stable

The rutschblock test can be adapted by non-skiers, using the same principle of a standard block size to which successive degrees of force are applied. If you are a snowshoer or snowboarder, the block could be slightly narrower than the dimensions given, but trench in the same distance on either side. The same is true for snowmobilers and others who can just jump on foot though if you are dealing with very soft or thin slabs that are easy to break through, it is recommended that you make a "fanny landing."

Banzai Jump Test

This test is a fun means of applying extra force to the snowpack to see if it will fail. As with the rutschblock test, it is also a great way to fill in your pit, keeping the slopes safe for others.

With a snow saw or ski, cut the shape of a trapezoid into the undisturbed area above the uphill pit wall. Ideally, you should saw through the potential slab and weak layer and into the likely bed surface. For a one person jump, the block should measure about 5 feet (1.5 meters) wide at the bottom, 4 feet wide (1.2 meters) at the top, and these cuts should be roughly 4 feet (1.2 meters) apart. The reason for making the test block trapezoidal is so that the block will be free-sliding and not "hinge" on the adjacent flanks. For each additional person, add approximately 1.5 foot (.45 meters) in width and length so that the uphill side of the trapezoid remains roughly the width of the jumpers. For five jumpers then, the length and uphill width of the block would be approximately 10 feet (3 meters) and the block would be slightly wider on the downslope side. The concept is to keep the block a standard size relative to the amount of body force applied.

The procedures with this test are similar to those of the rutschblock in that the testers apply increasing amounts of force to the test block. As a group, stand just above the uphill cut and tightly interlock arms at the elbows so that you can keep a good grip on each other. On cue, the whole group should flex their knees, applying a slight amount of force to the apex area of the cut. If the block does not fail, do a coordinated jump on the count of three, yelling "banzai" in mid-air, and landing on an imaginary line drawn across the upper third of the block. If you are in an area with sharp rocks or the snow surface is very hard, land on your feet even though it is sometimes more difficult to distribute the stress this way. Otherwise, it is preferable to do a fanny landing. If the block does not fail, try not to slide into the pit but instead, do several more group jumps.

Some blocks will fail just as you are getting into position, others will not fail even when shock loaded through repeated jumps. As with other snowpit shear tests, the easier the slab fails, the more unstable the layer, all other things being equal. The results from your banzai test should help confirm or challenge the opinion you've developed thus far concerning snow stability. This test is safe as long as it is done on small slopes where the consequences of getting carried downslope are minimal and the group holds on to

Obviously, the banzai jump test needs to be performed only in safe locations, for example, at the top of a small slope with minimal exposure. To allow you to build a meaningful scale for interpreting your results over time, make your blocks consistently the same size for a given number of jumpers. Here, the test block is fracturing and sliding in response to one jump.

each other. The banzai test done at the top of small slopes without cutting out a block can be a good way to trigger slides as long as slab failure will not endanger the jumpers.

* * * *

These tests allow you to obtain a maximum amount of snowpack information in a minimum amount of time. It is very important that you conduct them *consistently*, making sure your blocks are the same size each time and that they are plumb. This will allow you to derive a meaningful scale so that you know what easy, moderate, and hard shears feel like and can relate your results to the stability of the snowpack.

The safest bet is to use snowpit and shear test results to tell you that the snowpack in a given area is unstable but not to tell you it is stable unless these results are well corroborated by other bull's-eye data. It cannot be overemphasized that while the tests provide you with one piece of information about snow stability at a given point, they cannot be used to solve the whole puzzle.

One of the best ways to eliminate uncertainty about the stability of a given slope is to try and make it avalanche before you get out onto it. These tests are potentially dangerous and must be conducted from a safe location at the top of the slope, preferably by experienced travellers using bombproof belays. Make absolutely sure that there are no travellers below you. Initially, practice these techniques on very small slopes, roughly 20-40 feet or 6-12 meters high.

The surface hoar pictured has been redistributed by gentle winds. After the next storm, snowpits dug several feet apart could yield very different messages concerning snow stability. Build your stability evaluation by integrating data from multiple sources.

There are a number of ways to try to cause slab failure. These include rolling large rocks or snow blocks onto the path from the ridge above (this is called trundling) or breaking off cornices which are also known as the "bombs of the backcountry." Cornices can be very dangerous and should be approached with *great* caution. They can extend long distances laterally and it is common for them to snap off much further back than anticipated. Avoid large cornices, instead favoring small, fresh ones. Rather than getting out onto a cornice, the best way to break off a section is to have two people, preferably standing on firm ground, loop a cord or climbing rope over the cornice and saw back and forth. Parachute cord or rope up to 1/4 inch (5 millimeter) in diameter works best and it can be helpful to tie knots in it.

Another method is ski-testing, that is, traversing slightly downslope across the top of a potential failure zone, from safe spot to safe spot while applying force into the snowpack. This test should be done only by expert skiers or snowboarders on small slopes with a spotter watching and only if the instability involves soft surface layers (as opposed to hard or deep slab instability). Do not attempt to ski cut large slopes. Make sure you are using releasable bindings.

Another possibility is to conduct a banzai jump test, unroped if the slope is very small with no serious hazards below, or belayed. Several important cautions are necessary here. The first is that when attempting a banzai jump test on a steep, convex slope, keep in mind that with every step you take over a convexity, the angle increases 2-3 degrees. The further you descend below the 35° mark, the greater the chances are of having the slope rip out above you. Be very careful not to drop too low on the slope--this is also a common mistake with ski-testing. Always jump *above* where failure is likely to occur, for example, start above the rollover. The force on a body caught in sliding snow can be tremendous. Belay anchor points can easily be pulled out, ropes broken, and/or testers injured or killed. Use solid anchors and belays and establish the belay station directly above the tester(s) so that they do not pendulum across the slope.

Recognize that even if you do not succeed in triggering an avalanche, the slope is not necessarily stable and may still fail when you attempt to travel on it. Maybe you did not apply enough force or affect the most sensitive trigger spot. Listen to what the other bull's-eye data is telling you.

Jumping on this short steep slope provided instant bull's eye feedback concerning snow instability. Choose low consequence, small test slopes and remember that the slope is not necessarily stable if it does not release. Maybe you didn't exert enough force or hit the tender spot.

67

WEATHER

IS THE WEATHER
CONTRIBUTING TO INSTABILITY?

Most *natural* avalanches occur during or shortly after storms because the snowpack often cannot adjust to the vast amounts of new weight added in a short time. Weather affects the stability of the snowpack by altering the critical balance between strength and stress. Let's consider how precipitation, wind, and temperature affect this balance.

PRECIPITATION (Type, amount, duration, intensity)

The significance of precipitation is that it increases the stress exerted upon the snowpack by adding weight. New snow or rain, especially heavy amounts, can make snow highly unstable. An important distinction between these types of precipitation is that new snow can provide a certain amount of strength to the snowpack through whatever bonding is taking place. Rain, on the other hand, adds weight *without* adding strength. Cold, dry snowpacks are particularly sensitive to rain. Heavy rain also helps weaken layers by warming them and eroding the bonds between grains as well as between slab layers. Though a wet snowpack may be extremely unstable, it can become very stable and strong when refrozen. The rain layers become icy crusts which can help tie the snow structure together. However, these crusts are discontinuities within the snowpack and a smooth crust can make a classic bed or sliding surface for future snowfalls.

How well the new snow layer bonds to the old snow surface is as important as the type and amount of precipitation that falls. Generally, rough, pitted, irregular surfaces allow for better adhesion than do smooth, glassy surfaces. For example, a thin layer of unconsolidated snow resting on top of a very smooth ice lens could produce extensive avalanche activity when buried by additional snowfall.

The surface rain runnels above are indicative of a snowpack which has been subjected to heavy amounts of rain. As the rain penetrates the snowpack, it often forms percolation columns (below) which channel the water downward until the water hits a denser, more impermeable layer and pools. Once refrozen, such snowpacks are extremely strong.

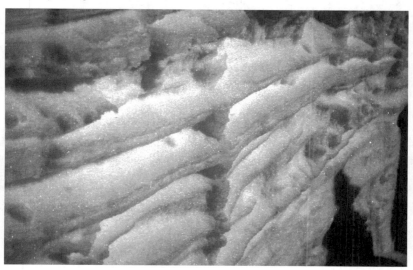

No stock answer exists concerning how much precipitation is required to produce instability and subsequent avalanching. Some storms drop several feet of new snow with little or no avalanche activity, while others may bring just four or five inches of new snow but result in widespread activity. This depends, in part, on the bonding qualities of the new snow as well as on the strength of the layers within the snow-pack. Generally, however, the most common cause of natural avalanches is increased load due to heavy amounts of precipitation or deposition of wind-transported snow.

The way in which the snowpack responds to load depends largely upon the intensity of the force (amount of loading) and the rate at which it is applied. Fast loading generally causes the snowpack to respond elastically, that is, when it is no longer able to store energy, it releases it suddenly and the snow fails in a brittle manner. This is similar to stretching a rubber band until it is stretched so far that it breaks. A slowly loaded snowpack generally responds by flowing, bending, and deforming, although failure may still occur, especially if deep slab instability exists. **The more rapid the loading, the less time the snowpack has to adjust to additional stress. In fact, any sudden change can be a stress on the snowpack.** All things being equal, two feet of new snow falling in ten hours is more likely to create unstable conditions than two feet of new snow falling over three days. Add wind and the problem is rapidly compounded.

WIND (Direction, speed, duration)

It can be a blue sky day but as far as the mountains are concerned, a storm is going on if the wind is blowing snow around. Wind is able to redistribute large amounts of snow by scouring windward slopes while rapidly loading leeward terrain and creating cornices. Because the wind breaks down snow crystals as they are bounced along the snow surface, wind-transported snow generally forms compact, often hollow-sounding, well-bonded layers. Depending upon wind speed and duration, the consistency of this snow can be soft or hard but either way, it often makes good slab material.

Wind direction is important because it determines which slopes are being loaded. For instance, strong southeasterly winds will predominantly load north and west-facing terrain. However, some loading will occur on all aspects as terrain features cause the wind to decelerate and drop snow. Wind-loading commonly occurs in several ways. Top-loading takes place when the wind blows over the top of a ridge, depositing snow just below ridge level. Generally, the stronger the wind, the further downslope the snow is deposited. Side-loading occurs when the wind blows across a slope, loading it on the leeward side of ridges or gullies bisecting the slope. Side-loading, also known as cross-loading, is sometimes more insidious because it can be harder to detect, especially in areas of gentle gullies. Furthermore, there may be a lot more snow from top to bottom that can be entrained in the slide.

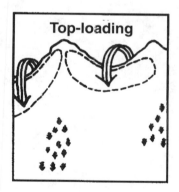

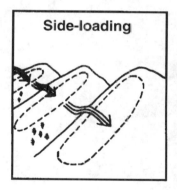

Note that while leeward slopes are becoming potentially more unstable due to increasing load, the stress on windward slopes is decreasing as the snow is stripped off. For this reason, windward slopes often make good routes. Beware though, because wind shifts in the mountains are common. Today's windward slopes may have been wind-loaded yesterday when they were on the leeward side of the prevailing wind. Also, the snow on predominantly windward slopes is often shallow, thus encouraging the development of weak, faceted grains. It is possible, though uncommon, for even heavily eroded windward slopes to produce fractures in which the wind-compacted surface snow breaks on the faceted grains underneath.

The wind speed required for snow transport depends partly on the snow surface type. For example, eight inches (20 centimeters) of loose, unconsolidated powder subjected to 15-20 mph winds (7.5-10 meters/second) would likely create highly unstable snow conditions within a couple of hours. Little transport and, thus, little change in stability would occur, however, if the snow surface consisted of a hard-packed old wind slab or an ice crust, even if the wind blew much harder. Finally, wind intensity and duration influence how quickly and how much stress is added or relieved on a given slope.

Wind is often responsible for changing snow stability within minutes or just a few steps. Note the sudden transition between wind-eroded snow on the left and the 3 foot (.9 m) drift to the right.

TEMPERATURE (Air/snow temperature and trends, solar/terrestrial radiation)

Changes in snow temperature can significantly affect snow stability. These changes are governed largely by ground and air temperatures, solar radiation, and terrestrial radiation, that is, reradiation from the earth's surface into the atmosphere.

An important concept is that the warmer the snowpack, the more rapidly changes within it occur, including metamorphism and deformation. A warm snowpack (above roughly 28°F or -2°C) ordinarily settles (compresses) rapidly, becoming denser and stronger. As it becomes denser, it also becomes more resistant to further densification. Periods of cloudy, moderate weather will encourage this rapid settlement process, often leading to greater snow stability in the long run, although avalanches will often occur during the warming process.

Settlement cones around obstacles such as shrubs and rocks are an indicator of how much the snowpack has settled since the last snowfall. As snow settles, it becomes denser and stronger and also more resistant to further deformation. Snow will settle more rapidly at warmer temperatures. What do these cones tell you about the stability of the snowpack? Not much. You still need to determine how well the new snow is bonded to underlying layers.

In a cold snowpack, unstable snow conditions often persist longer, sometimes for weeks or even months, because the settlement or strengthening process is slowed. In addition, the snowpack may be weakening very gradually through kinetic growth metamorphism as discussed earlier. This means that the weight or movement of a person on a given slope is sometimes enough to trigger an avalanche long after the actual storm or wind-loading event created potential instability. However, cooling of a warmed snowpack, that is, one that has been subjected to warm winds, rain, or solar radiation, to temperatures below freezing generally results in a more stable condition, all other things being equal.

The effects of warming of the snowpack can be double-edged. While gradual warming can encourage strengthening and stabilization through settlement, rapid, intense warming can make the snowpack more unstable by weakening the bonds between grains and increasing the rate of downslope deformation in affected layers. Because layers of different temperatures and densities flow downhill at different rates of speed (warm, less dense layers flow fastest), increased stress may result at the interface between warmed snow and colder layers underneath.

The amount of solar radiation absorbed by the snow surface depends upon the time of day and year, the extent of cloud cover, the latitude, the moisture content of the snowpack, and very importantly, the aspect, elevation, and angle of the slope. In addition to absorbing heat energy, snow radiates heat efficiently and can be cooled significantly by outgoing terrestrial radiation especially when the sky is clear. This surface radiation can be counteracted, however, by back radiation from warm cloud cover. This means that the snowpack can actually warm more rapidly in cloudy, warm conditions than under sunny skies at the same temperature. Likewise, a moist or wet snowpack warms at a faster rate than a dry one. Dry snowpacks typically reflect up to 90% of incoming solar radiation back into the atmosphere.

If the snowpack is able to warm gradually, for example, under conditions of temperate days and clear, cold nights during which the snowpack can refreeze, avalanche activity will typically be limited to surface layers. These warmed layers peel off much like an onion skin as loose snow slides and shallow slabs. Even when small, though, the debris in these slides can be much like a slurry of concrete. Some cornice breaks are also possible under these conditions. Given buried weak layers or discontinuities in the snowpack, prolonged warming can cause deeper slab releases. These are common particularly after several consecutive nights when the snowpack does not refreeze. It is not unusual for some of these deep slab instabilities to be triggered by loose snow slides or cornice breaks.

Sunballs (evident on the lower slope) indicate surface instability due to solar warming but tell nothing about what might be happening deeper in the snowpack. This clue is significant as an indicator of change and it is important to monitor how rapidly the snowpack is warming. Though the higher slope has the same aspect, no sunballs are present. Why? Apparently the colder temperatures of higher elevation have offset the effects of solar warming.

When dealing with a snowpack that is being subjected to significant warming, *timing* is critical. A slope that is hard and stable in the morning may produce avalanches by the afternoon as an ice crust is transformed into wet snow. Remember that a rapidly warming snowpack also weakens very rapidly. Travelling in springtime conditions is an art because it is easy to miss the short window between, for example, sensational, steep terrain skiing in 2 or 3 inches (5-8 centimeters) of warmed corn snow and potentially deadly skiing in ankle deep slush. Early signs that the snowpack in a given area is warming include a cupping texture on the snow surface and small snowballs (sunballs) rolling downslope. These clues do not necessarily mean that a slope has to be avoided but it is critical to monitor how fast the warming is penetrating into the snowpack. Note that avalanche activity often peaks several hours after the daily peak in solar radiation. For reasons that are not yet fully understood but appear to be related to contraction of the snow surface, it has also been observed that sometimes shallow, wet slabs release in the evening, just after a sun-warmed slope is over-taken by shadows.

The absence of warming on a slope throughout much of the winter can be as potentially hazardous as direct, intense sun. For example, on shaded slopes, the snowpack not only undergoes less (or slower) settle-ment due to warming but also the development of weak layers such as faceted snow or surface hoar is favored. This is because temperature gradients within the snowpack and at the snow surface can be more pronounced and persist for longer periods of time.

Lastly, air temperature trends during a storm are important because they affect layer strength and bonding. Storms that start out cold and get progressively warmer are more likely to produce avalanches than those that start out warm and progressively become cooler. The fluffy, cold snow that falls early in the storm often bonds poorly to the old snow surface and is not strong enough to support the denser snow deposited on top of it as temperatures warm. Conversely, relatively warm snow falling at temperatures of roughly high 20's to low 30's in °F (-3° to 1°C) often bonds well to the previously warmed old snow surface and strengthens rapidly through settlement. However, any rapid, prolonged rise in temperature following long periods of cold weather could potentially lead to instability and should be noted as one of nature's billboards.

In summary, weather is the architect of avalanches and as such it provides the blueprint for changes in snow stability. By anticipating the effects of weather conditions and changing weather patterns upon the structure of the snowpack, you can greatly increase your margin of safety as you travel through avalanche terrain.

These lenticular clouds are indicators of strong winds aloft. Always try to anticipate how the wind, an approaching storm, or other weather variables might affect the stability of the snowpack. (Photo by Nick Parker)

TYPICAL WEATHER PATTERNS RESULTING IN UNSTABLE SNOW CONDITIONS

❋ **Heavy amount of new snow loading in a short period.** *Result:* Increased stress due to rapid loading.

❋ **Heavy rain.** *Result:* Weight but no strength is added to the snowpack. Bonds between grains are eroded and weakened.

❋ **Long, cold, clear, calm period followed by heavy precipitation and/or wind-loading.** *Result:* Deposition of a slab over a weak layer (probably well-developed layers of faceted grains or surface hoar).

❋ **Storms that start out cold and end warm.** Or warm storms, with temperatures near the freezing level, that follow long periods (several days or weeks) of cold weather. *Result:* Development of an "upside-down layer cake." Instability is generally shortlived but sensitive.

❋ **Clear weather with strong winds causing significant snow transport.** *Result:* Rapid loading of leeward slopes, development of wind slabs, and cornice formation. Add a layer of powder snow over the slabs making them more difficult to detect and the probability of human-triggered avalanches becomes even higher.

❋ **Rapid and prolonged temperature rise to near or above freezing after a long period of cold weather.** *Result:* If the snowpack was previously stable, some surface instability may occur until temperatures cool. If weak layers exist within the snowpack, deeper slab releases are very possible and may be triggered by surface sluffing or cornice breaks.

❋ **Intense solar radiation, particularly with a thin layer of clouds above.** *Result:* Loose snow and slab avalanches may occur as surface layer(s) are likely to weaken rapidly. If deeper instabilities exist, deep slab avalanches could be triggered, again often by surface sluffing or cornice breaks.

THE HUMAN FACTOR

WHAT ARE YOUR ALTERNATIVES AND THEIR POSSIBLE CONSEQUENCES?

It is possible to travel at times of high snow instability by choosing safe routes (if they exist). Similarly, it is possible get caught in an avalanche during periods of relatively low snow instability through poor route selection and stability evaluation. In other words, we create potential *hazard* by travelling in avalanche terrain and we can determine what degree of hazard we face on any particular day given good decision-making. Thus far, we have discussed the terrain, snowpack, and weather variables that make it possible for a slope to avalanche. However, it is the "human factor" that *allows* avalanche accidents to happen. A discussion of the various human factors that most commonly get us into trouble follows.

ATTITUDE

Attitude is one of the main causes of avalanche accidents as it leads us to filter data and warp it to our needs and desires. What is your goal and what level of risk are you willing to assume to achieve it? In other words, identify your "yardstick for success." If your goal is to climb a new, very exposed route, all members of your group must be willing to accept a higher level of risk than a group heading outside to enjoy a beautiful day. Just make sure that the level of risk is clearly understood by all. Commonly, travellers are willing to assume high risk levels until someone gets injured or killed and then their actions no longer seem worth the consequences.

When you are considering travelling in risky terrain under marginal conditions, what you are really talking about is *"What's your attitude towards life?"* A strong physical and mental state is as likely to contribute towards an avalanche accident as a weak one, if your attitude is that of a high risk-taker. People with high risk-taking attitudes generally filter information about potential hazard and draw unrealistically

79

optimistic conclusions which lead them to push the fine line even finer. People who are generally conservative by nature tend to use the same information to further justify their conservative approach.

Keep in mind that nature does not care what you think. Conditions need to be evaluated objectively on their own merit. Thus, it is important for you to tune in to how your own attitude and that of your friends may bias your judgment.

ASSUMPTIONS AND CONSEQUENCES

Any avalanche hazard evaluation is only as good as the data on which it is based. Our decisions must be based on bull's-eye facts and observations rather than assumptions or feelings. Ask yourself: What assumptions am I basing my decisions upon? Always identify and check out your assumptions.

Examples of assumptions that can get you into trouble include:

"The forecast center said the hazard was low to moderate, so we didn't expect to get caught." Note: Make your own stability evaluations. Hazard forecasts are regional, not site-specific.

"We thought it was safe because there were already tracks on the slope." Note: Tracks on the surface of the snow do not tell you anything about the stability of the underlying snowpack. Slopes with over 150 tracks on them have slid. What is the terrain, snowpack, and weather data telling you about snow stability?

"It was a blue sky day with great new powder snow and no avalanches." Note: Every avalanche cycle must have its first avalanche event. While most natural avalanches happen during storms, including wind-loading events, the majority of human-triggered avalanches occur on the blue sky days after storms. This is because: 1) most people do not travel in white-out storm conditions and 2) the new load has

increased the stress on the snowpack and may or may not have caused natural releases depending upon the strength of the snowpack. When we go outside, hungry for new powder, our weight on or near steep slopes is often enough to tip the critical balance between stress and strength.

"I've travelled to this place a hundred times before and never seen an avalanche. There's nothing to worry about." Note: Most of the time, the snowpack is stable so we get positive reinforcement and begin to think of an area as safe. If the site is avalanche terrain and we travel there enough times, sooner or later we will be there when the snow is unstable.

"There was only 18 inches (46 centimeters) of snow so we didn't think the slope could avalanche." Note: There is no minimum amount of snow necessary to produce an avalanche. Integrate other key pieces of data including the slope angle and the roughness of the ground surface.

"We were wearing rescue beacons, so we figured we would be OK even if we got caught." Note: A functioning beacon just means that the beacon will be recovered at some point. Too many times, people wearing beacons have died from mechanical injuries during the ride, suffocated before they were dug out, and/or not been found quickly because the other members of the group were also caught or did not know how to search effectively. If you find yourself feeling reassured because you are wearing a transmitting beacon, maybe the real message is that you are in the wrong place at the wrong time and you need to take an alternative course of action.

"We planned the trip for six months and we weren't about to throw it all away because of one storm. Besides, it was our third try at climbing this mountain." Note: Timing is everything.

Again, nature is not concerned about our beliefs, schedules, or goals. It does not matter to an unstable slope that we are fatigued, that our ego is at stake, that we're suffering from tunnel vision, that we're afraid to look cowardly, that we're being subjected to peer pressure, that we're strong travellers, that we have to be back at work on Monday, or that darkness is approaching. In each of the previous examples, the victims ran into trouble because they presumed that a situation was safe or rationalized their decisions. Other human factors that commonly get mountain travellers into trouble include the "sheep syndrome," that is, blindly following whoever is leading, the "cow syndrome," a rush to get "back to the barn" at the end of the day, and the "lion syndrome," a rush for first tracks.

Your safety in the mountains requires that you evaluate avalanche potential from nature's perspective. Whenever you are on or near

Small but potentially deadly, this hard slab avalanche with debris weighing roughly a million pounds (453,600 kg) was triggered by a 100 pound (45 kg) woman doing a kick turn at the base of the slope. Many people assume such slopes are too small to avalanche, an assumption not based upon data.

steep, snow-covered slopes regardless of the slope size or time of year, you need to think like an avalanche.

Think about the potential consequences of your actions. What are your chances of success versus your chances of getting caught, buried, or killed? Is it worth it? Do better alternatives exist?

SKILL LEVEL/ PREPAREDNESS/ EQUIPMENT

Generally, two categories of people tend to get into trouble with avalanches: novices and experienced travellers. Novices fall within the category of "ignorance is bliss." When an accident happens, they are usually totally surprised and unprepared. They simply have not learned the basics of avalanche hazard recognition, evaluation, and rescue.

The bottom line question is what's going to happen if you get caught? (Photo by Bruce Tremper)

Experienced travellers tend to misjudge the hazard or overestimate their ability to travel through potentially hazardous terrain. Commonly, their travel skills (e.g., skiing, snowboarding, snowmachining, etc.) far exceed their ability to evaluate avalanche hazard. Yet often, other members of the group rely on this person to make the hazard calls.

Occasionally, being reasonably sure that you will not fall, or that you can travel quickly, or knowing that all members of the party have rescue equipment and are proficient with it will allow you to travel in marginal conditions. For example, a storm might be raging with snow instability increasing rapidly but not yet critical. Under the same circumstances, less experienced travellers would almost certainly get into trouble. In most situations, however, cutting the fine line like this will turn you into a statistic. Almost certainly, if you push this line often enough, the probability curve will eventually catch up with you. Experience is best used to recognize, evaluate, and avoid potential avalanche hazard.

HUMAN FACTORS WHICH ARE MAJOR CONTRIBUTORS TO AVALANCHE ACCIDENTS

- ATTITUDE
- EGO
- POOR PLANNING
- DENIAL
- TUNNEL VISION
- LAZINESS
- MONEY CONSIDERATIONS

- PEER PRESSURE
- INDECISION
- HASTE
- POOR COMMUNICATION
- COMPLACENCY
- SUMMIT FEVER
- FATIGUE

DECISION-MAKING: USING THE AVALANCHE HAZARD EVALUATION CHECKLIST

Skilled avalanche hazard evaluation is based upon a systematic decision-making process in which you:

❋ Identify potential problems.
❋ Continuously collect, evaluate, and integrate 🎯 data (facts, observations, and test results that have a high degree of certainty in their message).
❋ Explore your alternatives and their possible consequences.
❋ Make a decision followed by action.
❋ Re-evaluate your decision if necessary based upon new information or changing conditions.

Sound decision-making demands good communication between group members. Exchange information and suggestions freely. Evaluate each other's assumptions.

Decision-making is not always easy, but the process is fairly straight-forward and doesn't have to take a lot of time, particularly if you limit the size of your group. Don't walk into a trap just because you are afraid to express your opinion, thinking that others know more than you do.

If necessary, say "No, I don't think we should follow that route because..." Equally important, learn to accept a "no" from another group member. A "no" based upon facts is a very powerful tool with which to save lives.

In investigating avalanche accidents, it is striking how often party members identified a number of clues pointing to the instability that eventually got them into trouble and either chose to ignore the clues, filter the information or rationalize the message. The following avalanche hazard evaluation checklist is a summary of the bottom line questions that need to be asked and answered when evaluating avalanche hazard and making decisions.

Get in the habit of assigning each of the critical factors a risk level which can be thought of as green lights, red lights, and yellow lights.

Red lights: Danger, a hazardous situation exists.

Yellow lights: Be cautious, there is potential hazard, too much uncertainty, or conditions are deteriorating.

Green lights: It's OK, no hazard exists.

For example, a 39° slope is a red light terrain factor. However, if all the critical snowpack and weather factors are green lights, from the point of view of an avalanche, you have a green light to go do whatever you want on that slope. Taken by itself, each piece of information portrays an important but incomplete view of the whole. When integrated together, however, a more complete message starts to appear. Internalizing and using this checklist and looking at the data as red, yellow, or green lights could save your life, if you are willing to listen to the message. Continually re-evaluate your situation without letting your attitude persuade you away from the facts.

AVALANCHE HAZARD EVALUATION CHECKLIST

Critical Data		Hazard Rating*		
PARAMETERS:	KEY INFORMATION	G	Y	R

TERRAIN: *Is the terrain capable of producing an avalanche?*
		G	Y	R
-Slope Angle (steep enough to slide? prime time?)		[]	[]	[]
-Slope Aspect (leeward, shadowed, or extremely sunny?)		[]	[]	[]
-Slope Configuration (anchoring? shape?)		[]	[]	[]
Overall Terrain Rating:		[]	[]	[]

SNOWPACK: *Could the snow fail?*
		G	Y	R
-Slab Configuration (slab? depth and distribution?)		[]	[]	[]
-Bonding Ability (weak layer? tender spots?)		[]	[]	[]
-Sensitivity (how much force to fail? shear tests? clues?)		[]	[]	[]
Overall Snowpack Rating:		[]	[]	[]

WEATHER: *Is the weather contributing to instability?*
		G	Y	R
-Precipitation (type, amount, intensity? added weight?)		[]	[]	[]
-Wind (snow transport? amount and rate of deposition?)		[]	[]	[]
-Temperature (storm trends? effects on snowpack?)		[]	[]	[]
Overall Weather Rating:		[]	[]	[]

HUMAN: *What are your alternatives and their possible consequences?*
		G	Y	R
-Attitude (toward life? risk? goals? assumptions?)		[]	[]	[]
-Technical Skill Level (travelling? evaluating aval. hazard?)		[]	[]	[]
-Strength/Equipment (strength? prepared for the worst?)		[]	[]	[]
Overall Human Rating:		[]	[]	[]

DECISION/ACTION:

Overall Hazard Rating/Go or no go?   *GO* [ ] *or NO GO* [ ]

* HAZARD LEVEL SYMBOLS: R = Red light (stop/dangerous), G = Green light (go/OK), Y= Yellow light (caution/potentially dangerous).

LOOKING AT DATA OBJECTIVELY

Designating each piece of data as red, yellow, or green will help you take the subjectivity out of decision-making. As mentioned, a slope angle of 39° is a red light. That would automatically make the overall light for terrain a red unless we find, for example, that the slope has trees so thick that it is impossible for us to even travel through them. Indications of a green light snowpack include *lack* of clues indicating instability (e.g., no shooting cracks or whumphing noises, recent avalanche activity, hollow sounds, etc.), hard shears, and negative results when jumping, ski-cutting, or dropping cornices on small test slopes. Let's look at various combinations of red, green, and yellow lights in terms of the bottom line, can we go (green light) or not (red light)?

DATA	TERRAIN	SNOWPACK	WEATHER	HUMAN	GO/NO GO
	R	R	R	G	R
	G	G	G	G	G
HAZARD	R	G	G	G	G
RATING	G	R	R	G	G
	R	R	G	G	R
	R	G	R	G	G/Y
	R	Y	Y	G	Y/R

Key: R = Red light, G = Green light, Y = Yellow light.

Notice that in all of the scenarios above, we have assumed that the group is open-minded, strong, and competent and given the human factor a green light. In reality, it is often a yellow or red light. Still, if terrain, snowpack, and weather are all red lights, the answer to the question "go or no go?" is obviously a "no go" or red light. Similarly, if terrain, snowpack, and weather are all green lights, we can safely travel the slope.

Now suppose the terrain is red (e.g. 37°, leeward), the snowpack is red (e.g., 14 inches or 36 centimeters of new and wind-deposited snow, poorly bonded to the old snow surface) and the weather is a green (e.g., blue sky, no wind), do you go or not? The answer is a resounding STOP. Note that while this seems obvious, the majority of accidents occur during these conditions. In the same scenario, if the snowpack was green, you could have a safe day on that slope. In other words, if you are a good snowmachiner and want to play highmark on 40° slopes, you can do so safely as long as the snowpack, and preferably the weather, are green lights.

"We never thought it was steep enough to slide. It couldn't have been more than 10° where we were standing although it was really steep up higher. Then suddenly, the entire slope broke loose and came down on us. We had heard some whumphing noises earlier, but didn't realize the significance. The storm ended yesterday and the weather today was perfectly clear." Anonymous survivor. Interpretation: Terrain=Red, Snowpack=Red, Weather=Green: No Go.

Let's say, from a recreationist's point of view, it has been a terrible winter with very little snow. From an avalanche perspective, thin snow cover often means a weak snowpack of faceted grains. Now, finally a big storm has come in. You are desperate to get outside. The snowpack is trying to adjust to the increased stress that is being exerted upon it. This is where your attitude could get you into trouble. Take yourself to a place where you have a choice of slope angles. If you find that the snowpack is a red, you simply have to notch the terrain back from a red to a green. You can have a great day playing on slopes with angles in the low 20's where there is high instability but no hazard because these slopes, and the ones they are connected to, are not steep enough to slide. Just make sure you do not stumble onto red terrain.

If you have yellow lights, evaluate whether they are due to uncertainty or to the fact that conditions are changing for the worse. If uncertainty is the problem, see if you can gather more data to turn the light into a more definite red or green. If conditions are changing, monitor the rate of change.

One of the few situations in which party strength and travel abilities could make a difference is if the terrain is a red, and the snowpack is a green changing to yellow as a result of yellow or red weather conditions. Strong parties may be able to safely go quickly while for weaker parties, it is a red light situation. **When in doubt or when conditions are changing rapidly, be conservative in your hazard evaluation and route selection decisions, leaving a margin for error.** The greater your uncertainty or the greater the consequences of an error in your judgment, the wider the necessary margin.

Remember that the purpose of seeking information is to reduce or eliminate uncertainty. The purpose of reducing uncertainty is to have a clear picture of the hazard. **The mountain environment is not static and potential hazard can, and often does, change within a matter of a few minutes or literally, a few feet.** Stay alert for clues and integrate terrain, snowpack, and weather data every step of the way.

TRAVELLING SMART: ROUTE SELECTION AND SAFE TRAVEL PRINCIPLES

Careful route selection can greatly reduce your chances of getting caught in an avalanche and in some areas, make it possible for you to travel during periods of high instability. When in the mountains, you cannot necessarily travel in a straight line. Sometimes whether you go a few feet to the right or left can make a big difference with respect to your safety. The tenets of safe route selection are based upon the following three concepts:

* ❄ Prepare for the worst.
* ❄ Utilize the terrain to your advantage.
* ❄ Minimize your exposure time and use safe travel procedures.

PREPARE FOR THE WORST

Research your route before going in the field (this is most relevant for mountaineering trips). Identify potentially hazardous or crux areas as well as safety zones. Utilize aerial and oblique photographs, maps, and local knowledge. During your approach, view the route from as many perspectives as possible. Identify your alternatives.

Check the current and forecasted weather before you leave. Ask about expected precipitation (i.e., types, amounts, storm duration), freeze level, wind speeds and direction, and temperature trends. You can call the National Weather Service or if available, a regional avalanche forecast center. If you can, telephone someone living near the area for site specific, real-time observations.

Know the capabilities of your group. Are your partners capable of doing the trip or tackling the slope you have in mind? Do not be forced to split your group as this has led to a large number of accidents. Do not be afraid of reconsidering your plan. Establish and agree upon the purpose of your trip (e.g., have fun, reach the summit no matter what, etc.). Keep your groups small. Groups larger than 4-6 people tend to feel invincible and often have a difficult time making decisions quickly and keeping track of each other.

Prepare for emergencies: Necessary equipment usually includes a functioning brain, avalanche rescue equipment (shovel, beacon, and probe), and survival/first aid gear. You may choose to file a trip plan with a responsible person before leaving. Answer who, what, when, where, and how. Importantly, leave a reasonable amount of time for bad weather. On the negative side, trip plans have often trapped parties into poor decision-making and trying, against all odds, to make it back by the "deadline." Fear that a search will be launched is not justification for exposing a group to risk.

UTILIZE THE TERRAIN TO YOUR ADVANTAGE

For example, favor the windward sides of ridges, avoid lee slopes until you have had the chance to check them out, or stay well out in the valley bottoms away from avalanche-producing slopes. Measure slope angles!

You can become an avalanche victim by:

❋ ignoring slight but significant increases in slope angle (this is very easy to do when traversing or dropping over a convexity);

❋ travelling with steep slopes above and/or hazardous terrain traps such as cliffs, ravines, and creek bottoms below (think consequences!);

❋ forgetting that it is possible to trigger an avalanche from a low angle slope or a ridge as long as where you are standing is connected to avalanche terrain and sensitive instability exists;

❋ overlooking subtle changes in snow conditions caused by wind or sun due to variations in slope aspect;

❋ presuming that a summer trail is necessarily a safe winter route;

❋ crossing a slope at or below a high stress point such as a convex rollover;

* assuming tree-covered slopes are safe (remember, if you can travel through the trees an avalanche can run through them);

* travelling on top of or underneath cornices, particularly those which have been recently loaded or warmed (do not forget about cornice crevasses); and

* travelling on a slope that has not yet slid as opposed to using the nearby bed surface of a recent avalanche. If the slope has fractured near ridge level and has not re-loaded, the bed surface can be a very safe route up, down, or across.

Whether a given route is "good" or "bad" depends largely on the stability of the snow. The route pictured is potentially dangerous -- the slope has an angle of 38°, it is poorly anchored, leeward, and there is evidence of vegetative damage from previous avalanches. Under stable conditions, however, this route is perfectly acceptable.

MINIMIZE YOUR EXPOSURE TIME AND
USE SAFE TRAVEL PROCEDURES

Minimize the amount of time you are exposed to hazard by knowing your route, travelling as quickly as possible, and being skilled in your method of travel.

Safe travel procedures include exposing as few people as possible (preferably one) to potential hazard at a time while all other members of the party watch the exposed person from safe spots. This not only minimizes the number of people that will get caught if something goes wrong, thus maximizing your available rescue resources, but also reduces the stress exerted at one time on the snowpack. Do not travel above your partner. Do not travel out of sight of each other. Do not stop in the middle of or at the bottom of steep slopes. **Read this paragraph over--it could save your life.**

Many of the snowmachiner fatalities in the United States have occurred when one rider has stopped or gotten stuck at the bottom of a steep slope and a partner has swung around or highmarked above him. Skier accidents have happened when one skier has stopped to take a picture of the other descending toward him. If you have to stop, do so at the edge of a slope (beyond the flanks of the slab), where you have some protection from the terrain, or well beyond the runout zone of the path.

Always think about potential escape routes--have in mind your quickest exit from hazard because you will only have a split second to react. If using ski poles, do not wear the straps around your wrist and ski or snowboard with releasable bindings, preferably with no safety straps (brakes are fine). If you are caught in an avalanche and cannot shed your equipment, it can and probably will drag you down into the flowing debris.

If ascending: Favor gentle angles and the margins of slopes. Avoid long traverses with steep slopes above you. When possible, use ridge routes but remember that ridges can produce avalanches if the terrain is steep enough and beware of cornices. If you are on skis ascending a narrow ridge, you need to make your zigzags similarly narrow even though it means a lot of kick turns. Sometimes, climbing straight up on foot may be your safest, fastest line but this depends greatly on the snowpack as floundering in the snow or kicking steps can put a lot of stress into the snowpack.

A Note to Snowmachiners Who Play Highmark: Be aware that you are taking a much greater risk when approaching steep slopes from the bottom. You can increase your chances of keeping a game from turning into a nightmare by picking *windward* rather than leeward slopes. As discussed above, start out on the edge of a slope, on lower angles

A combination of new snow loading, steep slope angles, leeward aspect, poor route selection, and risky travel procedures resulted in this avalanche and the death of a snowmobiler playing highmark with his two partners. The weight of the machines and riders was all that was required to tip the critical balance between stress and strength within the snowpack.

rather than "center-punching" the slope or aiming for the steepest angles. Avoid terrain traps. Snowmachiners have been killed in avalanches where the fractures wrapped completely around a bowl and the debris, which funneled into a central depression, piled up more than 30 feet (9 meters) deep. Again, make sure that only one machine and driver are on the slope at a time, with all others watching from a safe location.

If crossing: Where possible, minimize your exposure by crossing on gentler slope angles or well out into the runout zone. If the slope is uniformly steep, you might want to cross as high as possible (if there are no terrain traps below), above the likely failure zone or at least where any moving snow has little chance to gain momentum before it reaches you. If using cliff bands for protection, stay high, close to the base of the cliffs where the snow may be more compacted and stronger because of sluffing off the rocks. Remember also that there may be stress concentration areas a very short distance below the rocks where the snow is able to flow downslope more freely. If the slope is too wide to keep your partners in sight, travel one at a time from safe spot to safe spot. Make sure the safe spots are really protected (e.g., a windswept ridge, anchors that you can grab without being swept away by moving snow from above). If possible, cross the slope at a slight downhill traverse to minimize your exposure time. Sometimes using the same traverse track will minimize disturbance to the snow as well as exposure time but this depends on the given snowpack. If you are nervous about crossing or there are no safe spots, find an alternate route or consider trying to trigger the slope before crossing.

If descending: If you want to travel on steep slopes, approach them from above whenever possible. Start by descending slopes with gentler angles and then as the day progresses, work your way onto steeper terrain. This gives you a chance to test your opinion about snow stability. It is often a good idea to favor the sides of a slope rather than the middle so that you have a better chance of escaping off to the side of a slab. Choose slopes where you can see the entire run and which have gradual, open runout zones rather than cliffs, gullies, or dense trees below. Be suspicious of steep rollovers or other potential tender spots such as rocky areas. Wherever you can, take advantage of natural protection such as some ridges or the bed surface of previous slides. If you're going to fall, try to sit rather than crash in order to minimize the size of the "bomb" (stress) you put into the slope. Have a plan which all members of the party agree upon. Decide which descent line the group will use on a given run. Make sure only one person descends the slope at a time while all others watch. Establish a safe stopping point. Have signals so that you are sure the exposed person is clear before the next person starts to descend. Finally, just in case, know the best escape route.

Know that sometimes there may be no safe route. If, however, you suspect instability on a route which absolutely *must* be descended, remember that you may have the option of trying to make the slope avalanche before you accidentally trigger a waiting trap. Continually reassess your alternatives as you almost always will have choices better than walking into the den of an angry dragon.

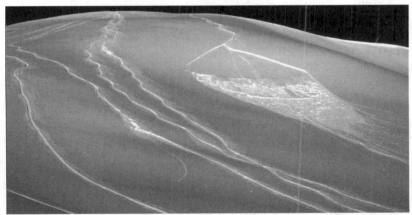

Sometimes, depending on the instability, a variation of only a few degrees in slope angle makes the difference between triggering a slide and avoiding the problem all together. The bed surface of this skier-triggered slab was 38° while the slope to the left was 35°. (Photo by Chuck O'Leary)

PUTTING IT ALL TOGETHER: MAXIMIZING YOUR SAFETY IN AVALANCHE TERRAIN

TIMING IS EVERYTHING. You can only travel safely on red terrain when the snowpack is a green. When instability exists, you need to notch back your slope angles.

MEASURE YOUR SLOPE ANGLES. This not only lets you know the capability of the terrain to produce avalanches, but also helps you categorize the type of instability you may be dealing with. For any given avalanche cycle or instability, failure will occur only on a certain range of slope angles. Keep in mind that shear failure propagation is common when a sensitive weak layer like surface hoar or young faceted snow is subjected to a new load.

ALWAYS LOOK FOR TENDER SPOTS OR AREAS OF STRESS CONCENTRATION. Likely problem areas are rollovers, places where the slope angle suddenly increases, wind-loaded areas, shaded aspects, thin spots, a short distance below cliff bands or near rocks and brush where weak layers are likely to be more well developed.

STUDY FRACTURE LINES. Note which slopes have slid, what the bed surface slope angles were, where the fractures broke, what they ran on, and how deep they were. You can learn a lot from this, including developing x-ray avalanche eyeballs for detecting tender spots and stress concentration areas. Also measure the runout or alpha angle, that is, the angle between the furthest extent of the avalanche and the fracture line. This angle is an indication of the runout distance or efficiency of a given avalanche. The lower the angle, the more efficient and longer-running the slide. If you have a path you like to travel in regularly, take a photograph of it and make an enlargement. Overlay the print with a plastic mylar. Draw any avalanche activity you observe during the season on this mylar and make a note as to contributory terrain, snowpack, and weather factors.

INTEGRATE CLUES. Continually seek bull's-eye data. Once you have an opinion about snow stability, keep seeking additional information to confirm or refute that opinion and to further reduce your level of uncertainty. Don't be "suckered" in by the absence of obvious clues like recent avalanche activity, whumphing noises, or shooting cracks. Your biggest clue may just be recent weather events.

HAMMER ON THE SNOWPACK. The snow stability evaluation process does not end until the snow melts. Do not get complacent. You can travel all day and find your problem spot within five minutes of the end of the day. Be very careful about climbing one aspect and travelling down another. Jump on little slopes. Cut cornices with ropes. Do belayed jump or pit tests. If you are an expert skier and are dealing with a surface instability, ski test small slopes when you have a good traverse line between safe spots and a reliable partner. If it does avalanche, take a few minutes to examine why. Keep in mind that just because a slope doesn't go, doesn't mean that it is stable.

ANALYZE YOUR ASSUMPTIONS / BEWARE OF THE HUMAN FACTOR. Remember that the avalanche dragons do not care if you are tired, hungry, grumpy, or late for work. Is your attitude interfering with your objectivity? When evaluating avalanche hazard, you need to think like an avalanche. Do not be reassured just because there are tracks on a slope.

CHOOSE YOUR TRAVEL LINES CAREFULLY. For your first run, choose a slightly less steep angle or a line off to the edge of the slope rather than center-punching the path. Always think escape routes. Which way are you going to jump if the slope cuts loose?

THINK CONSEQUENCES. What's going to happen to you if you get caught or buried? Do better alternatives exist? Is it worth it?

BE CONSERVATIVE. When in doubt, notch back your slope angles. If you have a "travel to die" attitude, you probably will.

USE SAFE TRAVEL PROCEDURES. Travel on or near steep slopes one at a time. Be anti-social. Never stop in the middle or at the bottom of an avalanche slope--always stop off to the side or well out away from the runout zone. Never travel above your partner. Keep each other in sight. Choose your partners carefully. If skiing, use releasable bindings and do not wear safety straps on your skis or poles.

BE PREPARED FOR THE WORST. Have a rescue plan and carry avalanche rescue equipment (shovel, beacon and probe per person). Understand that your beacon is not a safety talisman. A functioning beacon just ensures that the beacon will be recovered and does not guarantee that you will survive the avalanche.

Get in the habit of trying to piece together the contributory causes of avalanches you observe. If possible to do so safely, examine fracture lines and measure the bed surface slope angles. Studying avalanches that have run will help you get a handle on current snow instability and improve your avalanche hazard evaluation skills.

LOOKING AHEAD

You have several choices in your approach to winter travel in the mountains. You can hone your travelling abilities, without working much on your avalanche hazard evaluation skills. By doing so you are essentially playing Russian roulette with nature. Most of the time you spin the chamber, you will win but the consequences of losing can be severe. Or, conversely, you can become completely paranoid about every snow-covered slope and never be able to travel anywhere because you are always deep in a snowpit. Best yet, you can arm yourself with knowledge. The way we see it, learning how to evaluate avalanche hazard is an investment in your future.

This book is a start. You can build on your avalanche hazard evaluation skills in a number of ways. When you are travelling, tune in *all* of your senses so that you are receptive to the messages the mountains are transmitting. Go out with experienced travellers and listen, learn, and question. Read more books. Go to a top quality avalanche workshop, taught by avalanche specialists, with field-oriented training. Keep a notebook in which you record weather observations, related avalanche events, or comments about the snowpack. Investigate avalanches that have released, trying to piece together the contributory causes of failure. Measure slope angles frequently with your inclinometer and record the angles of your favorite slopes. Study the snowpack in a given area to see how the layers change over time. Keep learning and never become complacent. To paraphrase Andre Roch, a Swiss pioneer of avalanche science, "Remember, the avalanche does not know you are an expert." Our bet is that the return on your investment is that you will enjoy the mountains more than ever and be able to elude the avalanche dragons. Good luck and have fun!

ADDITIONAL INFORMATION: AVALANCHE RESCUE

The best avalanche rescue strategy is not to get caught in the first place because avalanche rescue does not work very well. Statistically, one out of every three people who gets caught and completely buried in an avalanche will die. If you travel alone or without essential safety equipment and/or have not formulated and practiced a rescue plan, you are greatly limiting your chances of survival if caught in an avalanche. **You do not have time to go for help. YOU ARE THE HELP!**

Essential equipment for each member of a party to carry *and* know how to use includes:

❧ Avalanche rescue transceiver (beacon)
❧ Avalanche probe or probe ski poles
❧ Shovel

An *avalanche rescue transceiver or beacon* is a small electronic device capable of transmitting and receiving a signal within a range of approximately 50 to 150+ feet (15-45+ meters). For the duration of a trip, each member of the group wears their beacon on their body (tucked inside their clothes) in transmit mode. Should an avalanche bury a member of the party, survivors switch their beacons to receive mode, spread out across the debris, and begin the search for their partner using a standard search pattern. A beacon is not directional; the signal will sound louder, the closer the searcher is to the buried beacon. Once a signal is picked up, the location of the buried beacon can usually be pinpointed within 2-4 minutes by a skilled searcher.

People wearing beacons have been killed by avalanches, even when dug out quickly, and beacons are little more than body locators if all members of a party are buried. However, they offer the greatest chance of recovering a completely buried person alive. It does not do your partner any good if you are wearing a beacon but do not know how to use it to search. Beacons are simple to use but proficiency requires *practice, practice, and more practice.* Beacons are expensive but so is most outdoor gear. A beacon might just save your life.

Probes are generally 8-10 feet (2.5-3 meters) long and are made in sections that can be fitted together. Some specially made ski poles also double as avalanche probes. If probes are not available, skis, ski poles, branches, etc. may be used although they are not nearly as effective. Without a probe, it is impossible to thoroughly check out surface clues, to confirm the location of a buried person wearing a transmitting beacon (you will waste a lot of time digging if you are off by even a small distance), or to conduct a probe line for a completely buried person who is not wearing a beacon.

Shovels move snow roughly five times faster than your hands. The average depth of burial for avalanche victims in the U.S. is just over 3 feet or 1 meter. There are a number of good one and two piece light-

Basic avalanche rescue equipment for each person in the party includes a shovel, probe, beacon and brain, all in operating order.

weight, aluminum shovels with medium-size scoops. It may not matter if your buried partner is wearing a beacon if you don't have a shovel, because you probably won't be able to dig him or her out in time anyway. It is helpful to rig your shovel with a rope or bungee cord that runs from the handle to a hole drilled at the top of the scoop. This will enable you to sling it over your shoulder or onto your back while you are searching the debris, thus guaranteeing that you have your shovel with you when you need it.

* * * *

Here's a brief summary of the essentials of a backcountry rescue plan, both as a victim and a rescuer.

RESCUE PLAN
As a Victim

❄ If you are caught in an avalanche, call out so other members of your party know to watch you as you are carried down the slope, and then keep your mouth closed to prevent ingestion of snow. You may have a split second to grab a tree, dig into the bed surface, or lunge, ski or "goose" your machine off to the side. If so, do it! (Note: If you are inside a vehicle when caught, immediately shut off the engine to avoid the danger of carbon monoxide poisoning.)

❄ If possible, discard cumbersome gear such as skis, ski poles, and pack (if it is heavy) although this is much easier said than done. This gear tends to drag you underneath the surface of the moving debris. You might, however want to keep a light pack with you as it may help protect your back and the gear in it will probably be useful in an emergency situation.

❄ Use a swimming and rolling motion to try to stay on the surface of the snow and/or work your way to the side of the avalanche. FIGHT with all your effort. You will likely be out of control but try to keep your head upslope and your feet downslope and maneuver around fixed objects like trees and rocks. The main message is that now is the time to struggle to stay on the surface and to avoid hitting objects which can inflict mechanical injuries.

✳ As you feel the snow slow down, thrust your hand or any part of your body above the snow surface so it can be seen by others. You probably will be so disoriented that you won't know where the snow surface is so just guess and lunge.

✳ Before the snow comes to rest, cup your arm or hand in front of your face to clear an air space. If possible, try to expand your chest during this time. A number of buried snowmachiners have credited their survival to the air space provided by their helmets.

✳ If buried, stop fighting and relax to preserve oxygen. Remember, you are not supposed to panic! Occasionally, buried victims have been found by yelling for help but usually the hearing of the rescuers is impaired by static such as the wind, rustling clothes, the sound of footsteps, etc. Victims can often hear more clearly because of the absence of this static under the snow. It is probably best to save your breath and yell only if you hear someone directly overhead.

As a Rescuer

✳ Watch the victim as he/she is carried down the slope. If the victim disappears under the moving snow, keep your eyes fixed on the mass of snow he/she was enveloped in, until it comes to rest. The victim may be under the snow surface in that area.

✳ Use the STOP and GO method. STOP means Stop, Think, Observe, Plan. GO means Go into action and Organize the rescuers. Do not panic! You are the victim's best chance of survival now. Stay on site and search. Almost all hope of a live rescue depends on you. Statistically, a victim has only about a 50% chance of survival if buried 30 minutes. The first 15 minutes are critical. Outside help cannot usually arrive fast enough. You are dealing with a drowning person!

A Note Concerning Not Going for Help: A person buried under the snow needs air immediately, not hours later. If you have a party of four and you send one person for help, you are losing 25% of your search party. Think of how much searching you can do in a half hour or hour! One exception would be if help can be summoned without depriving the victim of your immediate aid (e.g., calling on a radio or cellular phone) and another might be sending for assistance after hours of intense searching. Keep in mind that it often takes hours for help to arrive on scene. If you go for help, you are usually going for a body recovery, not a rescue.

✳ Before entering the search area, make sure there is no further avalanche danger along your approach route or at the site and pick a quick escape route understood by all. If the avalanche was human-triggered or occurred on a small slope, rescuers can probably go into the slide area safely, especially if they enter the path on snow that has already slid. If nearly all of the starting zone has released and no loading is taking place, it is highly unlikely that it will avalanche again. If it is storming or windy, observe the rate at which reloading is occurring. If a significant portion of the starting zone has not released and loading is still occurring, the possibility of a second avalanche may be high. The debris will not slide again but be careful of situations where multiple release zones funnel into a single runout zone or where other people approaching from above might trigger a release. Responding to an avalanche rescue can be extremely dangerous or fatal to rescuers who travel with disregard for existing avalanche hazard. If necessary, use your checklist to evaluate the conditions and do not hesitate to halt the search if red lights are flashing.

✳ Take a *few* moments to organize the search party. Delegate tasks, be systematic and efficiently allocate your resources. Do not scatter gear belonging to the rescuers in the search area or you will soon confuse it with possible clues.

✳ Mark the area where the victim was last seen above the snow and search downslope of this area. The last seen area, clues on the surface, and the fall-line may help establish the victim's downslope trajectory. If you can limit the likely search area, you greatly increase the chances of a successful search.

✳ If you respond to an avalanche which has been witnessed by someone else, question the witness and if at all possible, return to the accident site with them. The witness is the most important clue you have regarding the number of victims, their last seen locations (or the relative location of each victim, including the witness, when the avalanche occurred), and whether or not the victims were wearing beacons.

✳ Your *initial search* should consist of:

Thoroughly searching for clues, such as a snowmachine ski sticking out of the snow or a hat on the debris. Clues may be very subtle. They could include entry or exit tracks, drops of blood, a piece of hair, a bit of ski pole basket, a dark area between snow blocks, a muffled scratching sound, or the family dog sitting in one location. Check out *all* clues by pulling on them and probing around them. Leave the clues in place (mark them if they are hard to

An obvious clue. Don't forget to also look for the more subtle ones.

see) and alert the other members of your party of their existence. **Move fast but take the time to look and listen carefully and be sure to cover the ENTIRE search area.**

Spot probing likely areas, including around clues, where snow is piled against protruding obstacles like trees or rocks, benches (dips, bowls, bends, etc.) where the snow has come to rest, or places where the slope angle decreases or the debris deposits are suspiciously thick. Spot probing, also known as random probing, means searching for a buried victim by pushing an avalanche probe vertically into the snow. The procedure is random in the sense that no particular grid pattern is used but you need to systematically search likely spots. The "golden rule" of probing is "probe onto others as you would have them probe onto you." In other words, do not jam the probe into the snow but push it steadily through the layers. The danger of hurting someone with a probe is less than the danger of the victim running out of air. If you wonder what it will feel like to probe a body, take a probe and poke yourself or better yet, a friend. Springy branches and unfrozen ground can feel like a body. When in doubt about a possible strike, check it out! Always have a shovel with you.

Conducting a beacon search of the entire deposition area, unless it is positively known that the victim is not wearing a beacon. Make sure that *all* rescuers have switched their beacons to receive. If you are wearing a beacon, you should already have practiced with it many times and be very familiar with standard search procedures, including bracketing and keeping your beacon oriented. After pinpointing the signal, probe to confirm the victim's exact location before digging.

✳ If the victim is not located after a very thorough initial search of the entire search or deposition area, begin a coarse probe in the most likely catchment area. Spread out, in a horizontal line, with rescuers elbow to elbow, hands on hips. If you are tall, draw your elbows in a bit. This is called a *closed coarse probe line.* Probes should be held vertically

The first responders to an avalanche accident have spread out across the debris and are systematically searching the entire deposition zone. Their initial search consists of looking and listening for clues, spot probing likely catchment areas, and conducting a beacon search.

and directly in front of each person so that the probes are 30 inches (76 centimeters) apart. Advance upslope 28 inches (70 centimeters) at a time. Move the probe first, then step up to it. It is best to move the line uphill as it is easier to keep the spacing together and a bit gentler on the backs of the rescuers. This grid spacing, which represents a compromise between thoroughness and the speed necessary to maximize the chances of recovering a victim alive, yields roughly a 76% probability that the victim will be found on the first pass. The probability of encounter increases slightly with each pass. It is important that the grid spacing be maintained, otherwise you are just taking a lot of time to do a "random probe." The verbal commands, preferably spoken by one person at the end of the line are "down probe, up probe, advance." Keep the line moving!

A closed coarse probe line in action during a formal rescue. Note that the rescuers have deposited their gear off of the avalanche debris so that it does not get confused with possible clues.

If you only have a few searchers, you can conduct an *open coarse probe line* which uses the same grid spacing (30 x 28 inches). Stand in a line across the slope, with both arms outstretched and your fingertips touching those of the person next to you. Again, if you are tall, draw your arms in slightly. With your feet shoulder width apart and angled outwards (at about a 45°), probe first off your left foot and then off your right foot before advancing. Commands are "on the left, down probe, up probe; on the right, down probe, up probe, on the right advance." Always advance on the side where you have just finished probing--it is easier to judge 28 inches straight ahead than diagonally.

All probe lines should work fast, efficiently, and quietly. If you are sure that you are probing the right area, after you have completed a pass, offset your line (to the left or right, whichever makes more sense) and probe it again. If you think, but are not absolutely sure that you have probed the buried person, leave your probe in place, have a second person quickly check it out, and immediately begin digging. If you are uncertain, always investigate by digging. When you drop out of the line, the rest of the probe team should close in the spacing and keep advancing until your find is confirmed. Otherwise, a great deal of time can be lost while digging out false strikes. If you do not find the victim in the primary search area after multiple passes, at some point you may need to expand the search area to include the next most likely area and repeat the steps above.

❋ When you locate a victim, dig fast but carefully and take care not to trample the victim's air space. If possible, excavate the person's head and chest first. Rather than "yanking" them out of the hole, conduct a careful primary and secondary survey. Treatment for suffocation, hypothermia, mechanical injuries, and/or shock is commonly required.

* * * * *

How long do you search? Continue searching until you find the victim, all hope is lost or until the hazard to rescuers is too great because of, for example, exhaustion, hypothermia, or increasing avalanche hazard. Darkness alone is not a reason to call off a search. Give the victim the benefit of the doubt! Some victims have been dug out dead after only a few minutes but some have lived for many hours and, under exceptional circumstances, even for days.

Common mistakes in avalanche rescues include: poor organization (e.g., no rescue plan, uncertain leadership, lack of rescue gear) and conducting an inadequate initial search (e.g., not doing one, not searching the entire area, not locating clues or probing likely spots, not knowing how to use a beacon). An initial search is also known as a hasty search. We discourage use of the latter term because it seems to promote the above errors which often result in a body recovery rather than a successful rescue. An initial search must be *both* thorough and fast.

Being able to respond effectively in a crisis situation, requires preparation. Have a rescue plan. The first time you and your partners discuss rescue should not be after something has already gone wrong. Practice beacon searches regularly. Once a week, all winter long is not too often; twice a year is too little. Organize and run probe lines. Set up simulated rescue scenarios to which you or your partners respond. Have some of these be surprises. Whenever possible, practice all the elements of rescue on avalanche debris.

Many people who have been buried say that one of the most frightening parts of their experience is when they are being dug out because their rescuers are standing on them and trampling their air space. Also, be aware that patients will cool rapidly as they are excavated from the snow.

SUMMARY OF THE NECESSARY
COMPONENTS OF A SUCCESSFUL RESCUE

Having a plan (knowing how & where to search)
Speed tempered with *safety*
Leadership
Communication
Efficient allocation of resources
Qualified searchers
Necessary equipment
First aid/evacuation
Self-help!

The best rescue strategy is not to get caught in the first place. The "moment of truth" pictured is one to be avoided.

113

RESOURCES FOR FURTHER LEARNING

The lists below are not comprehensive, but they are a start. * Indicates books that may be ordered from the Alaska Mountain Safety Center, Inc. which also offers beacons, probes, shovels, snow saws, and inclinometers, all at discounted prices.

SUPPLEMENTARY READING

Armstrong, B. and K. Williams, 1992, revised edition. *The Avalanche Book.* Fulcrum, Inc., Golden, Colorado, 240 pages. *

Daffern, T., 1992, 2nd edition. *Avalanche Safety for Skiers & Climbers.* Rocky Mountain Books, Calgary, Alberta, Canada, 192 pages.

LaChapelle, E.R., 1969. *Field Guide to Snow Crystals.* University of Washington Press, Seattle, Washington, 101 pages. Reprinted by the Journal of Glaciology, Cambridge, England.

LaChapelle, E.R., 1985. *The ABC of Avalanche Safety.* Mountaineers Books, Seattle, Washington, 112 pages.

McClung, D.M. and Schaerer, P.A., 1993, *Avalanche Handbook,* Mountaineers Books, Seattle, Washington, 271 pages.*

Perla, R.I. and M. Martinelli, Jr., 1978, *Avalanche Handbook.* U.S. Department of Agriculture Handbook 489, U.S. Government Printing Office, Washington, D.C., 254 pages, (out-of-print).

Roch, A., 1980. *Neve E Valanghe.* Club Alpino Italiano, Milan, Italy, 268 pages, (in Italian).

Salm, B. 1982. *Lawinenkunde für den Praktiker.* Schweizer Alpen-Club, Switzerland, 148 pages, (in German, also available in Italian).

Stethem, C.J. and P.A. Schaerer, 1980. *Avalanche Accidents in Canada II, A Selection of Case Histories of Accidents 1943 to 1978.* National Research Council of Canada, Paper No. 926, Vancouver, British Columbia, Canada, 75 pages.

Valla, F. 1991. *Ski et Securite.* Glénat and Association Nationale pour L'Etude de la Neige et des Avalanches, Grenoble, France, 127 pages, (in French).

Williams, K. and B. Armstrong, 1984. *The Snowy Torrents, Avalanche Accidents in the United States, 1972-79.* Teton Bookshop Publishing Company, Jackson, Wyoming, 221 pages. *

114

Also: *The Avalanche Review.* Periodical published 6 times yearly. For subscription information, contact: American Association of Avalanche Professionals, P.O. Box 34004, Truckee, CA, 96160, (916) 587-3653.

AVALANCHE HAZARD EVALUATION TRAINING
USA/CANADA (For other schools or countries, inquire locally):

Alaska Avalanche School
Alaska Mountain Safety Center, Inc.
9140 Brewsters Drive
Anchorage, AK 99516
(907) 345-3566 (workshops in AK & western U.S.)

American Avalanche Institute, Inc.
P.O. Box 308
Wilson, WY 83014
(307) 733-3315 (workshops in western U.S.)

Back Country Avalanche Institute
P.O. Box 1050
Canmore, Alberta T0L 0M0, Canada
(403) 678-4102

Canadian Avalanche Association Training School
P.O. Box 2759
Revelstoke, B.C., VOE 2SO, Canada
(604) 837-2435

National Avalanche School
National Ski Patrol System, Inc.
133 S. Van Gordon St., Suite 100
Lakewood, CO 80228 (school held every 2 years)

Northwest Avalanche Institute
1 Crystal Mountain Blvd.
Crystal Mountain, WA 98022
(206) 663-2597 (workshops in Washington and Oregon)

MOUNTAIN WEATHER AND SNOW STABILITY INFORMATION
Consult your local telephone directory and, if available, list the avalanche forecast number in your area here:_____

NOTES